CRISIS LEADERSHIP

Planning for the Unthinkable

Chris Kayes

This book focuses on a broad overview because it is precisely the Big Picture that is missing in nearly all of the current books on Crisis Management. Most books zero in on detailed topics such as Business Recovery, i.e., how to get a business back on its feet after a crisis. While such books certainly cover the details, they fail to show how the various "parts" fit together into a more "coherent whole."[4]

In addition, many important topics such as Stakeholder Analysis have been treated in a cursory manner in this book. This is certainly not because the topic is unimportant. Indeed, it is vitally important. Rather, I have treated the topic extensively in previous books.[5] The reader is referred to these with regard to the details of Stakeholder Analysis. The purpose of this book is to show where Stakeholder Analysis fits into the general framework of Crisis Leadership.

In sum, this book is more about the general philosophy of Crisis Leadership than it is about the technical details. Unless the philosophy is understood first, the details will make little sense.

ACKNOWLEDGEMENTS

I am indebted to far too many people to mention every one of them by name. I would, however, like to single out Warren Bennis, Ralph Kilmann, and Dick Mason. They are true friends and colleagues in the best sense of the term. They have helped in the formulation and the execution of this book in more ways than I could possibly acknowledge.

I also wish to note that this book is the result of a unique collaborative relationship. Specifically, I owe a tremendous debt to my former as well as my current students. I have learned more from them than I wish I could have taught them.

In particular, I would like to single out the USC Crisis Group, whose members are: Dr. Judith Clair, Dr. Sarah Kovoor, Dr. Maria Nathan, Dr. Thierry Pauchant, and Dr. Chris Pearson. In addition, the following doctoral students are also members: Mr. Murat Alpaslan, Mr. Chris Bresnahan, and Ms. Laura Farmer Hawkins. While the USC Crisis Group certainly does not agree with every word and thought that is expressed in this book, they nonetheless have influenced every part of it. I gratefully acknowledge their contributions.

I also wish to acknowledge the years of collaboration with Mr. Gus Anagnos. I also want to thank my secretary, Ms. Terry Scott, for all of her help.

NOTES

1. Kilmann, Ralph H., *Quantum Organizations: A New Paradigm for Achieving Organizational Success and Personal Meaning,* Palo Alto, CA: Consulting Psychologists Press/Davies-Black Publishing, 2001; see also Adler, P. S., and Borys, B., "Two Types of Bureaucracy: Enabling and Coercive," *Administrative Science Quarterly,* 1996, 41: 61–89; Bartlett, C. A., and Ghoshal, S., "Managing Across Borders: New Strategic Requirements," *Sloan Management Review,* 1987, 7–17; Bartlett, C. A., and Ghoshal, S., "Beyond the M Form: Toward a Managerial Theory of the Firm. *Strategic Management Journal 14* (special issue), 1993: 23–46; Burns, L. R., "Matrix Management in Hospitals: Testing Theories of Matrix Structure and Development," *Administrative Science Quarterly,* 34: 349—368;1957; Johnson, G. V., and Tingey, S., "Matrix Organizations: Blueprint of Nursing Care Organization for the 80's, *Hospital and Health Services Administration,* 1976, 21(1): 27–39; Ouchi, W. G., "Markets, Bureaucracies, and Clans," *Administrative Science Quarterly,* 1980,

25: 129–141; Ouchi, W. G., *Theory Z,* New York: Avon, 1981; Schein, E. H., *Organizational Culture and Leadership,* San Francisco: Jossey-Bass, 1985; Thompson, J., *Organizations in Action: Social Science Bases of Administrative Theory,* New York: McGraw-Hill, 1967.

2. Ackoff, Russell, *The Democratic Corporation: A Radical Prescription for Recreating Corporate America and Rediscovering Success,* New York: Oxford University Press, 1994.

3. For instance, see Elliott, Dominic, Swartz, Ethne, and Herbane, Brahim, *Business Continuity: A Crisis Management Approach,* New York: Routledge, 2002.

4. See Covello, V. T., Sandman, P. M., and Slovic, P., "Risk Communication, Risk Statistics and Risk Comparisons: A Manual for Plant Managers," Washington, DC: Chemical Manufacturers Association, 1988; Doswell, B., *Guide to Business Continuity Management,* Leicester: Perpetuity Press, UK, 2000; Hiles, A., and Barnes, P. (eds.), *Business Continuity Management,* London: Wiley, 1999; Kuong, J., and Isaacson, J., *How to Prepare an EDP Plan for Business Continuity,* Wellesley Hills, MA: Management Advisory Publications, 1986.

5. See Mitroff, Ian I. and Linstone, Harold A., *The Unbounded Mind: Breaking the Chains of Traditional Business Thinking,* New York: Oxford University Press, 1993.

second place. I would go even further: the same mentality that created our problems cannot be used to formulate, or state, them correctly, let alone solve them.

In large measure, our problem is caused also by the fact that our educational system is as fragmented as the organizations we have constructed. In fact, the organizations directly reflect what we teach and how we teach it. For instance, despite the fact that the technical and the human aspects of all problems are completely intertwined, we act as if they are independent can be contained and managed in separate departments or disciplines. Indeed, we persist in teaching scientific, technical, and human subjects in altogether separate university departments. In this sense, our educational system is a significant part of the problem we face. It is certainly not the solution.

Walk into almost any organization today. If it even has a Crisis Management, not to mention a Crisis Leadership, function or program, then more likely than not it will be highly fragmented. The responsibilities for Crisis Management will be split among myriad corporate functions such as Legal, Security, Manufacturing, Finance, and Public Affairs. The fragmented nature of Crisis Management directly reflects how we have designed organizations.

For years, I have taught courses in individual and organizational behavior. I have also taught courses in Crisis Management and critical thinking. No matter what the particular course, however, I have attempted to integrate the concepts that are used in each of them.

Far too many courses in individual and organizational behavior are taught as if the various topics are independent of one another. As a result, very few texts provide a framework that shows how, where, and why all of the topics fit together as an whole. This lack of integration prevents students from forming an integrative "roadmap" of the material. The result is that students are unable to see how the various topics relate to one another. This also means that they are unable to use them in an integrated and coherent manner.

This book exists to correct these and other defects. It can be used in a variety of ways. First of all, it can be read as a self-standing textbook on Crisis Leadership. It can also be used as a supplementary text in courses on Organizational Behavior and Crisis Communications. It can also be used in executive programs on Crisis Leadership and General Management. It can also be used in a wide variety of courses at both the undergraduate and the graduate levels in psychology, sociology, and philosophy.

Since I have not presupposed that the reader is familiar with complex organizations or crises, I have written the book for a wide audience. In this way, the book can be read by the general public, certainly by those who are interested in why crises happen. Since crises affect everyone, all of us need to understand why they occur and what can be done to lessen their occurrence and impact.

Most of all, I have written this book to give readers a comprehensive framework so that they can understand the multitude of factors and forces that need to be considered in framing an effective program of Crisis Leadership.

Because it is so important, I want to emphasize that the primary purpose of this book is to give the reader a *broad overview* of Crisis Leadership so that he or she can understand the general nature of Crisis Leadership. For this reason, it deliberately avoids discussing many important topics in detail.[3]

PREFACE

THIS BOOK HAS THREE MAJOR OBJECTIVES:

1. To explain *what* effective Crisis Leadership is;
2. To explain *why* effective Crisis Leadership requires organizations that are effective, and vice versa; and,
3. To present a *compact* and *integrated* model of human behavior that applies equally to individuals and to organizations.

Today's organizations are the result of a distinct and specific set of historical forces. These forces have combined to produce organizations that are highly fragmented. This fragmentation affects every aspect of their operations.

Despite the fact that we live in a world where increasingly everything interacts with everything else, we persist in designing and managing organizations as if they were machines. Even worse, we are managing extremely complex and highly interactive systems as if they were simple machines.

Machines have the quintessential property that they can be broken apart into independent components. For instance, when corporate functions such as Legal, Public Affairs, Finance, Marketing, and Production are put into self-standing departments with little or no substantial contact between them, then we are acting as if organizations are machines. We also do this when different products and geographical regions are put into different operating divisions and units. The result is that most organizations still are run as if they were nothing more than independent, self-standing silos, i.e., machines. This is the case despite the fact that years of research have demonstrated unequivocally the superiority of alternate ways of designing and managing organizations.[1]

All of this flies sharply in the face of globalization. Traditional geographic time zones and political boundaries are irrelevant. To take but one example, information flows freely across countries and organizational units according to its own "logic" and pace. For another, whether they start in a particular region of the globe, or with a particular product or brand, all crises quickly become global. That is, they quickly escalate to affect the home organization and major brands.

On every front of our existence, we have produced a world that is a complex, interconnected, and interdependent *system*. There are no aspects of our lives that are not firmly planted in the Systems Age.[2]

One cannot emphasize too strongly that the fundamental problem is that we are trying to manage the problems of the Systems Age with a Machine Age mentality. As Albert Einstein observed over fifty years ago, the same mentality that is responsible for creating our initial problems in the first place cannot be used to solve them in the

Chapter 12

THE VITAL IMPORTANCE OF SPIRITUALITY IN CRISIS LEADERSHIP **103**

Chapter 8

CRISIS LEADERSHIP AND THE MYERS-BRIGGS **68**

Chapter 9

THE ROLE OF CONFLICT IN CRISIS LEADERSHIP **74**

Chapter 10

AN EXPANDED VIEW OF SIGNAL DETECTION **81**

Chapter 6

THE DIFFERENT LANGUAGES OF MANAGERS AND EXECUTIVES: THE PERSONALITIES OF INDIVIDUALS   **41**

Chapter 7

THE PERSONALITIES OF ORGANIZATIONS   **56**

Chapter 4

THE FAILURE OF CONVENTIONAL RESPONSES 23

Chapter 5

THE RISE OF ABNORMAL ACCIDENTS: A BRIEF HISTORY OF CRISES 33

TABLE OF CONTENTS

Acquisitions Editor *Jeff Marshall*
Assistant Editor *Jessica Bartelt*
Marketing Manager *Charity Robey*
Managing Editor *Lari Bishop*
Associate Production Manager *Kelly Tavares*
Production Editor *Sarah Wolfman-Robichaud*
Illustration Editor *Benjamin Reece*
Cover Design *Jennifer Fisher*
Cover Image *Artville*

This book was set in Times by Leyh Publishing LLC and was printed by Courier Corporation. The cover was printed by Phoenix Color Corp.

Copyright © 2004 by John Wiley & Sons, Inc.

ISBN: 0-471-22918-0

Printed in the United States of America

10 9 8 7 6 5 4 3 2 1

CRISIS LEADERSHIP
Planning for the Unthinkable

Ian Mitroff
University of Southern California

⊗WILEY

www.wiley.com/college/mitroff

ABOUT THE AUTHOR

Dr. Ian Mitroff is the Harold Quinton Distinguished Professor of Business Policy in the Marshall School of Business at the University of Southern California. He also holds a joint appointment in the School of Journalism in the Annenberg School of Communication where he is the co-director of the USC Center for Strategic Public Relations. In addition, he is the President of Comprehensive Crisis Management, a private consulting firm specializing in the treatment of human-caused crises.

In 1986, Dr. Mitroff founded the USC Center for Crisis Management in the Graduate School of Business at the University of Southern California. He served as director of the Center for ten years. Under the direction of Dr. Mitroff, and with the support of the USC Graduate School of Business and major corporations, the Center has become an acknowledged national and international leader in the field of Crisis Management.

Dr. Mitroff holds a B.S. in Engineering Physics, a M.S. in Structural Mechanics, and a Ph.D. in Engineering Science, all from the University of California at Berkeley. He is the author of over 250 papers and articles as well as 22 books, including *The Essential Guide to Managing Corporate Crises: A Step-By-Step Handbook for Surviving Major Catastrophes* (Oxford University Press, New York, 1996). He is also a frequent contributor to the Op Ed pages of the Los Angeles Times and National Public Radio's Marketplace.

CHAPTER 1

INTRODUCTION—PEOPLE, TECHNOLOGIES, AND CRISES

In the daily hunt for targets near the Taliban stronghold of Kandahar, Navy pilots receive valuable assistance from what might once have seemed an unlikely source: Army air controllers in Afghanistan.

For half a century, Pentagon doctrine has preached cooperation among all branches of the military. That goal has often proved elusive. The competition between the Army and Navy, for example, is not limited to an annual football game between their two academies.

Source: Tony Perry, "Wartime Benefit: Services Cooperating," *Los Angeles Times,* December 4, 2001, p. A5.

Chernobyl, the Gulf War, Ford/Firestone, the World Trade Center and Pentagon bombings, Enron, and unfortunately, the most recent, the tragic destruction of the space shuttle, *Columbia:* these are only a few of the names that come readily to mind when one mentions the word "crisis." This book is about why crises happen, and what, if anything, can be done to manage them better, if not prevent them altogether.[1]

ORGANIZATIONS, PEOPLE, TECHNOLOGIES, AND CRISES

Figure 1.1 is a greatly oversimplified diagram of the relationships between organizations, people, technologies, and crises. Although the diagram is deliberately simplified, its purpose is to convey the fact that all technologies are designed and operated by people. In turn, the overwhelming majority of people work in organizations consisting of at least two or more people. Generally speaking, the more complex the technologies, the larger the organizations in which they are operated. But this means that people and organizations are responsible for the introduction of errors, both unintentional *and* intentional, into the operation of technologies.[2] The inevitable results are major crises.

TECHNOLOGIES

Technologies allow humans to accomplish things that they could not otherwise. The first, and perhaps the most basic, contribution of all technologies to human beings is that they magnify and extend the five senses.

1

FIGURE 1-1 The Relationship between Organizations, People, Technologies, and Crises

They allow us to see microscopic things or things at great distances that we cannot see with the unaided, naked eye. They also magnify sounds and heighten our taste buds' sensitivity. They not only allow us to smell faint odors but to tolerate noxious ones as well. They also increase the sensitivity of our touch.

Technologies also allow us to do things that are beyond human capabilities, such as to fly and to lift enormous weights. In addition, technologies not only protect us from difficult and dangerous environments, but also allow us to operate safely within them. In this way, they insulate us from dangerous operating conditions.

In short, technologies allow us to transcend physical, geographical, and time limitations. In addition, when their costs plummet, as is the case with electronic calculators, they also help us transcend economic limitations in that they become more readily available to a wider market of users. Finally, technologies also allow us to exceed the natural limitations on our cognitive and mental abilities.

If the sciences and the technologies extend and magnify our *senses,* then in contrast, the humanities and the social sciences extend and magnify our *sensibilities.* The humanities and the social sciences increase our ability to witness and to appreciate new experiences. They increase not only our capabilities but also our capacities to experience human emotions. They also allow us to experience a wider array of human experiences. Ideally, they allow us to place our thoughts and our actions in a wider context.

In sum, for our purposes, a technology may be defined as anything that:

■ *Magnifies, intensifies, or increases* the human senses (for example, microscopes, automobiles, hearing aids, telescopes) so that humans can accomplish tasks that would be virtually impossible without their assistance; for instance, to "see" atoms or to travel at high speeds;

- *Magnifies, intensifies, or increases* the human muscles and/or skeletal structure so that humans can accomplish tasks that would be virtually impossible without them; for example, to lift great weights, to ski down treacherous mountains;

- *Protects and insulates* humans from dangerous and difficult operating conditions (fires, outer space);

- Allows humans to *perform* exceedingly complex tasks in short time periods, for instance, to carry out millions, and even billions, of calculations per second via computers; and

- Allows humans to *carry out and to operate* complex tasks more safely and more efficiently than they could without them, for example, to produce energy from nuclear power plants.

Notice that none of these aspects or functions is necessarily independent. Indeed, one or more of them normally occur simultaneously, such as when someone places a "telephone call" and arranges a TV transmission signal to an orbiting space shuttle.

Why Major Crises Occur

In every case, a major crisis results when there is a serious breakdown, or malfunction, between people, organizations, and technologies.[3] As we shall see, a major crisis exposes a series of faulty, underlying assumptions that we have been making, and thereby taking for granted, about people, technologies, and organizations. In short, a crisis invalidates nearly every one of the critical assumptions individuals, organizations, or even whole societies have been making about people, organizations, and technologies. (We shall say more about this in Chapter Eleven.)

As important as technologies are, in this book our primary focus is on people, organizations, and crises. Unless they are given proper consideration and treatment, the characteristics, or the properties, of people and organizations interact strongly to produce major crises.

PEOPLE

People differ greatly in their skills and personalities. This includes their styles of making decisions, their underlying personalities, how they respond to and handle conflicts, how their ego and defense systems are organized, how they handle and respond to difficult people, cope with anger, and, perhaps the most important of all, how they develop their loftiest goals and impulses that we label spiritual.

Although people are exceedingly complex, we are going to show nonetheless that a relatively straightforward framework can be used to analyze them. For our purposes, we are going to look at people through three major lenses:

- Their personality or decision styles;
- How they handle and respond to conflict (i.e., their different styles of handling conflict); and

■ Their different "ego" states.

ORGANIZATIONS

Organizations enable people working in groups to accomplish goals that none of them could do on their own. In this way, they are able to harness complex, and simple, technologies to achieve shared goals.

Organizations transform raw materials into finished products and services. They accomplish this by putting people into different work groups such that they can work toward a common objective. Of course, organizations do many additional things as well. For instance, they raise capital or resources so that they can establish manufacturing and production capabilities. They also recruit people with the special skills needed to develop and to operate the technologies they employ.

If people are complex, then organizations are equally so. For our purposes, organizations can be characterized in terms of:

■ Their general business policies and strategies;

■ How they organize different tasks into jobs;

■ The kind of structures they have, for instance, the number of levels they contain and whether they are arranged hierarchically;

■ Their reward systems (i.e., what they reward and why; conversely, what they discourage); and

■ The kinds of communication channels they contain and sanction.

CRISES

Crises can be analyzed in terms of the following four key factors:

■ *Crisis types*—There are various, distinct "kinds" of crises. These fall into a limited number of distinct categories or "families." The particular set of crises an organization chooses to prepare, or conversely, to neglect, constitutes its Crisis Portfolio.

■ *Crisis mechanisms*—Crisis mechanisms include early warning signal detectors, damage control systems, and business recovery systems. As we shall see, this factor is exceedingly important because virtually all crises send out warning signals long before they occur. If these signals can be picked up and acted upon, then many crises can be prevented, the best possible form of Crisis Leadership.

■ *Crisis systems*—Crisis systems include how an organization is structured, how many levels it has, and how they are arranged. This in turn affects whether the organization's structure either facilitates or inhibits effective Crisis Leadership; in other words, the structure affects how quickly and efficiently early warning signals are passed up and down the organization. Crisis systems also include one of the most important variables connected with an organization (i.e., its culture or underlying "personality").

- *Crisis stakeholders*—Crisis stakeholders are all of the various parties, institutions, and even societies that affect and are affected by a major crisis.

As we shall see, what differentiates Crisis Leadership (CL) from Crisis Management (CM) is that CL recognizes the need to manage these four factors *before, during,* and *after* a crisis. The "before" phase of CL consists of performing a pre-crisis audit of the strengths and vulnerabilities of an organization. It also involves the development of the actual skills and capabilities needed to manage a crisis. The "during" phase involves the enactment of pre-crisis capabilities. That is, it does *not* consist of mechanically following crisis plans. The "after" phase involves a reassessment of one's crisis performance so as to design and to implement new CL procedures that will be more effective in meeting future crises. We shall say much more about each of these four factors and the before, during, and after phases of CL.

CONCLUDING REMARKS

There are enormous, complex interactions between organizations, people, technologies, and crises. Nonetheless, it is possible to discuss all of these critical "variables" in an organized, systematic fashion such that at the end of this book the reader will have a coherent framework to make sense of all of them.

EXERCISES

1. Give as many definitions as you can of the term "crisis." What are the differences between your definitions? Would some definitions be more appropriate for some organizations and not others? Why?

2. List as many types of crises as you can. Do they fall into different categories or types? Why? Are there certain types of crises that every organization should prepare for? Neglect?

3. List as many functions of different technologies as you can. Do technologies do more things than were listed in this chapter? Why?

4. Outline separate scenarios as to: how the improper operation of a technology can lead to a major crisis; how a poor organizational structure can lead to the unsafe operation of technologies.

5. List as many interactions as you can between people, organizations, and technologies that can result in crises.

6. Expand on the differences between Crisis Management and Crisis Leadership. In particular, expand on the activities that are necessary to prepare an organization "before" an actual crisis hits it. Also, expand on the critical activities that an organization needs to execute "during" and "after" a major crisis.

NOTES

1. Barton, L., "Terrorism as an International Business Crisis," *Management Decision,* 1993, 31(1): 22–25; Billing, R., Milburn, T., and Schaalman, M., "A Model of Crisis Perception," *Administrative Science Quarterly,* 1980, 25: 300–316; Keown-McMullan, C., "Crisis: When Does a Molehill Become a Mountain?," *Disaster Prevention and Management,* 1997, 6(1): 4–10; Lee, R.G., and Russo, R J., "Dealing with Disasters Takes Careful Planning Ahead of Time," *Building Design and Construction,* 1996, 37(9): f37–38; Mitroff, I.I., and Anagnos, G., *Managing Crises Before They Happen: What Every Executive and Manager Needs to Know About Crisis Management,* New York: AMACOM, 2000; Mitroff, I.I., Pearson, C. M., and Harrington, L.K., *The Essential Guide to Managing Corporate Crises,* New York: Oxford University Press, 1996; Mitroff, I.I., and Pauchant, T.C., *We're So Big and Powerful Nothing Bad Can Happen to Us: An Investigation of America's Crisis Prone Corporations,* Secaucus, NJ: Vol. Carol Pub. Group, 1990; Mitroff, I., Pauchant, T., and Shrivastava, P., "The Structure of Man-Made Organization Crises," *Technological Forecasting and Social Change,* 1988, 33: 83–107; Mitroff, I.I., Shrivastava, P., and F. Udwadia, "Effective Crisis Management," *Academy of Management Executive,* 1987, 1(3): 283–292; Newman, L.N., "Lessons From Bridgestone/Firestone," *Business and Economic Review,* 2001, 47(2): 15, 4; Pauchant, T., and Douville, R., "Recent Research in Crisis Management: A Study of 24 Authors' Publications from 1986 to 1991," *Industrial and Environmental Crisis Quarterly,* 1993, 7(1): 43–66; Perrow, C., *Normal Accidents: Living with High Risk Technologies,* New York: Basic Books, 1984; Perrow, Charles, "The President's Commission and the Normal Accident," in D. Sills, C. Wolf, and V. Shelanski (eds.), *The Accident at Three Mile Island: The Human Dimensions,* Boulder, CO: Westview Press, 1981, 173–184; Schwartz, H., "On the Psychodynamics of Organizational Disaster," *Columbia Journal of World Disaster,* 1987, 22(1): 59–68; Shrivastava, P., *Bhopal: Anatomy of a Crisis,* New York: Ballinger, 1987; Shrivastava, P., and Mitroff, I., "Strategic Management of Corporate Crises," *Columbia Journal of World Business,* 1987, 22(1): 5–11; Smith, R., "Planning for Contingencies," *Industrial Management and Data Systems,* 1996, 96(6): 27–28; Starbuck, W., Greve, A., and Hedberg, B., "Responding to Crises," *Journal of Business Administration,* Spring 1978, reprinted in J. Quinn and H. Mintzberg (eds.) *The Strategy Process,* Englewood Cliffs, NJ: Prentice Hall, 1992; Starbuck, W.H., and Milliken, F.J., "Challenger: Finetuning the Odds Until Something Breaks," *Journal of Management Studies,* 1988, 25: 319–340; Turner, B., and Pidgeon, N., *Man-Made Disasters,* 2nd ed., London: Butterworth-Heinemann, 1997; Turner, B., "The Organization and Interorganizational Development of Disasters," *Administrative Science Quarterly,* 1976, 21: 378–389; Vaughan, D., "Autonomy, Interdependence and Social Control: NASA and the Space Shuttle Challenger," *Administrative Science Quarterly,* 1990, 35: 225–257; Weick, K.E., and Sutcliffe, K.M., *Managing the Unexpected: Assuring High Performance in an Age of Complexity,* University of Michigan Business School Management Series, San Francisco: Jossey-Bass, 2001; Wildavsky, A.B., *Searching for Safety,* New Brunswick, NJ: Transaction Books, 1988.
2. Clair, J.A., "Turning Poison into Medicine: A Grounded Theoretical Analysis of Processes, Pathologies, and Designs in the Detection of Potential Organizations Crises," Unpublished Dissertation, University of Southern California, Los Angeles, 1993; Herman, C.F., "Some Consequences of Crises Which Limit the Viability of Organizations," *Administrative Science Quarterly,* 1963, 12: 61–62; Keown-McMullen, op. cit.; Kovoor, S., "Crisis Preparation in Technical Organizations: A Study Using a Multi-Dimensional Approach," unpublished dissertation, California, Los Angeles, 1991; Mitroff and Pauchant, 1990, op. cit.; Mitroff and Anagnos, op. cit., Mitroff, Pauchant, and Shrivastava, op. cit.; Newman, op. cit.; Perrow, 1984, op. cit.; Seeger, M.W., and Ulmer, R.R., "Virtuous Responses to Organizational Crises: Aaron Feuerstein and Milt Cole," *Journal of Business Ethics,* 2001, 31(4) 369–376; Schwartz, 1987, op. cit.; Shrivastava, 1987, op. cit.; Staw, B.M., Sandelands, L.E., and Dutton, J.E., "Threat-Rigidity Effects in Organizational Behavior: A Multilevel Analysis," *Administrative Science Quarterly,* 1981, 266(4): 501–525; Turner, 1997, op. cit.; Turner, 1976, op. cit.; Weick, K.E., "The Collapse of Sensemaking in Organizations: The Mann Gulch Disaster," *Administrative Science Quarterly,* 1993, 38, 628–652; Weick and Sutcliffe, op. cit.
3. See notes 1 and 2.

CHAPTER 2

THE FAILURE OF CONVENTIONAL THINKING

Counterterrorism experts and government officials interviewed by TIME *say that for all the relative calm since Sept. 11, America's luck will probably run out again, sooner or later. "It's going to be worse and a lot of people are going to die," warns a U.S. counterterrorism official. "I don't think there is a damn thing we are going to be able to do about it."*

Source: Massimo Calabresi and Romesh Ratnesar, "Can We Stop the Next Attack?" *TIME,* March 11, 2002, p. 26.

In the next four chapters, we are going to examine various factors and institutional forces that are responsible for the rise of crises. In this chapter, we examine primarily the failures of conventional thinking, especially as it is currently embodied in Risk Management.[1] We will also examine some of the critical differences between Crisis Management and Crisis Leadership.

A TALE OF TWO COMPANIES

The following two stories are real. Only the names of the individuals and the companies have been changed in order to protect them from attack. In today's world, these fears are unfortunately as important and serious as the stories themselves.

Magnitron

Janet Warren is the chief legal counsel of Magnitron, a U.S. Fortune 1000 company that makes highly specialized equipment for the chemical industry. At the request of Jeff Rivers, Magnitron's CEO, she has called a meeting of the heads of Security, Public Affairs, Marketing, Manufacturing, Finance, Operations, etc., to review Magnitron's Crisis Management plans and procedures.

Approximately a year prior to September 11, 2001, Magnitron has essentially done what most organizations have with regard to Crisis Management. (Notice that at best the case of Magnitron illustrates Crisis Management, not Crisis Leadership. As we proceed, we will make clear the critical differences between Crisis Management and Crisis Leadership.) Magnitron's executives have reexamined the crises that they have experienced over the last five years. For each crisis, such as defective or substandard products, they have examined how many times each has occurred. They have also calculated the cost of each actually occurring crisis, as well as each "near miss," i.e., those situations that came dangerously close to being a crisis but for whatever reason were averted, such as the near collision between two aircraft in flight. As a result, they have a frequency count of all the actual crises such as workplace violence, fires, explosions, threats to the computerized information databases, etc., as well as how much each has cost. The crucial point is that they have done this analysis *only* for those crises that have already occurred.

Based on this data, they have prioritized the list of crises for which they need to prepare. To perform this prioritization, they have *multiplied* the frequency with which a particular crisis has occurred in the past by its average cost. The resulting number (product) is the "average expected cost" of a particular crisis. Finally, they have ranked the resulting numbers from the largest to the smallest.

This way of calculating and ranking risks is basic to the field of Risk Management. In order to find the "average" or "expected cost" of a particular crisis, one merely multiplies the frequency with which a particular crisis has occurred times its average cost. (Think of it this way: If one has an "unbiased" coin, then the probability that on any particular toss it will come up heads is equal to 50 percent. The same is true for tails. This is indeed the definition of "an unbiased coin." Thus, in a hundred tosses of a quarter, we would expect to get fifty heads and fifty tails. Suppose further that every time the quarter comes up heads, we win one dollar, and every time it comes up tails, we lose one dollar. The total amount of money we would expect to make on average for one hundred tosses is: $50 \times \$1 + 50 \times -\$1 = 0$.)

Ms. Warren is chairing a meeting to review Magnitron's Crisis Management plans and procedures.

> *Janet:* According to the data before us, product defects are the number one crisis we have to worry about. Since this responsibility falls primarily on the shoulders of Quality Assurance, I have asked Karen Steele to tell us about what she has been doing to improve our procedures in the area of QA.

> *Karen:* Thanks, Janet. I am pleased to say that we have undertaken a thorough review of all of our QA procedures. As a result, we have lowered product defects from 2 percent to under 1/10 of 1 percent. But we are not satisfied. Quality is a never-ending process. It's a constantly moving target. We'll never be completely satisfied until we reduce our defects to where we are substantially better than anyone else in our industry. Even this won't completely satisfy us, but we're constantly working toward it.

> *Janet:* If there are no additional concerns, I'm going to close the meeting. We all have a lot to do. Does anyone else want to raise anything before we close?

> *Bob Toritteali, head of Security:* I know that I may be a worrywart, but I'm getting very concerned about terrorism. We've never had a terrorist incident per se. Nonetheless, there have been signs that incidents that

could be classified as terrorism have been breaking out in ancillary industries. It's true that they can't be completely identified as such, but they are close enough that I am beginning to really worry. I don't have any solid data to go on, but I wonder whether we should seriously consider the possibility of terrorism striking us.

Janet: Bob, I appreciate your concerns. But as you've said, it hasn't happened to us yet, and you don't have any solid data to go on.

As a result, I don't think terrorism needs to be our number one priority. I don't even think it needs to be on our radar screen. The chances of anything like this happening to us are very remote. We can't afford to spend our time and energy worrying about everything that might possibly happen.

I want to thank all of you again for your time. If anything out of the ordinary occurs, we'll reconvene this committee. Until then, I don't see any need to waste our time.

Ameridyne

Ameridyne is also a U.S. Fortune 1000 company. It manufactures health products. It has recently been in the news because one of its drugs, Ameridahl, has been "associated with" serious health problems.

Although there is no conclusive scientific evidence linking Ameridahl with serious illnesses, the number of consumer complaints with regard to problems experienced as a result of taking the drug has risen to a level such that it has made headlines in every major national publication and radio and TV news show. Even though Ameridahl represents only 1 percent of Amerdyne's total sales, the effect on the entire company has been substantial. As the result of negative publicity, Amerdyne's sales have taken a 20 percent drop across the board.

Amerdyne's CEO, Joe Talbort, has called a meeting of his Risk Management Committee. Because of the gravity of the situation, he is chairing the meeting himself.

Joe: I am here today because of the seriousness of the situation we're facing. All of you know the facts. All of you know what's happened over the past year. Whether Ameridahl is or is not at fault is not the reason why we're here. Although there's still no conclusive scientific evidence that there is anything wrong with Ameridahl, nonetheless we are facing a crisis because the public believes that there is something wrong with it.

I'm not here to place blame because that won't help us. What I want to do is to review the ways in which we have thought about potential threats and crises in the past. Like just about everybody else we have practiced Risk Analysis. However, because of what's happened, I no longer have any faith in this procedure.

As you all know, Ameridahl represents only 1 percent of our business. Therefore, if we followed the "logic" of traditional Risk Management, we should multiply 0.01 times the expected profits from

Ameridahl to arrive at the average expected negative consequences to the company.[2] This way of reasoning, I believe, is seriously faulty. It did not take into account the negative spillover effects that would accrue to all of the products in our company in the case where one product, however minor it might be in our total sales, were to suffer negative customer reactions. In the future, I am no longer going to rank the impacts of crises using traditional Risk Management. I am going to rank crises solely in terms of their *total impacts* on the entire organization, i.e., their *total costs,* irrespective of their probabilities of occurrence.

However, this raises a very thorny issue. What in God's name are we going to do in order to assess the impact of crises we know about, let alone those we haven't even thought of?

THE STATE OF CRISIS MANAGEMENT

These conversations are anything but hypothetical. Unfortunately, the first company, Magnitron, represents the vast majority of discussions that occur in corporate America with respect to Crisis Management. Based upon all the surveys and the interviews that we have conducted over the past 20 years, Magnitron is typical of at least 85 to 90 percent of the discussions that occur in corporate and government America. On the other hand, Ameridyne is typical of at best only 10 to 15 percent. The vast majority of organizations and institutions, public and private, are nowhere near as prepared as they need to be for major crises.

The differences between these two companies illustrate the differences between Crisis Management and Crisis Leadership. Crisis Management is primarily *reactive.* It addresses crises only *after* they have happened. On the other hand, Crisis Leadership is *proactive.* It attempts to identify crises and prepare an organization systemically, i.e., as a whole system, *before* a major crisis has happened.

What is so remarkable is that after September 11, 2001, not much has changed substantially. Those organizations that followed traditional Risk Management procedures, procedures that we now believe are inadequate to the task of Crisis Leadership, persist in using them. They have still not gotten the point that after September 11, 2001, the world has changed fundamentally. As a result, new thinking of the highest order is called for.

As unbelievable as it may be, the state of affairs is even worse. Unlike Magnitron, most companies are not prepared even for the crises they experience most often! What is it about the human condition that not only prevents us from preparing for the *thinkable,* let alone the *unthinkable?* It is one thing to deny crises such as terrorism altogether. But what is it that allows us to deny that which is directly in front of us?

A Massive Failure

For most people, the events that occurred in New York City, Pennsylvania, and Washington, DC, on September 11, 2001, are, thank God, utterly unthinkable. In fact, most of us would probably prefer *not* to think about them at all. And yet, even though we will always be unable to prevent such atrocities completely, if we are to lower substantially the odds of occurrence of "future unthinkables," then we have no alternative but to improve dramatically our abilities to "think about the unthinkable."

The tragedies not only represented the massive failure of our institutions to pick up threats of terrorism, but even more they represented the failure of the thinking that has laid behind the design of our institutions. It represented the failure of all of our institutions to think and to act critically.

The ability to think critically is the very essence of "thinking about the unthinkable." In turn, the ability to think critically demands the following:

- The ability to be aware of, to examine, and to challenge one's fundamental assumptions about the world;
- The ability to "connect the dots," i.e., to see the "big picture"; and,
- The ability to think "way outside the boxes" of conventional thinking.

If we are to redesign our institutions so that we will have a much greater chance of anticipating and preparing for future crises, then we have to alter fundamentally the ways in which we think about critical issues. As we noted in the Preface, Albert Einstein pointed out that the kind of thinking that is responsible for the creation of our problems cannot be used to define them, let alone solve them. With great foresight, Einstein also noted that the invention of nuclear weapons, which ushered in the Systems Age, had changed everything except our mechanistic modes of thinking.

The Differences Between Conventional and Critical Thinking

The differences between conventional and critical thinking can be illustrated by comparing the crashes of ValuJet Flight 592 on May 11, 1996, and TWA Flight 800, on July 18, 1996. In the case of ValuJet, all 110 people aboard died when an airliner crashed into a swamp in Florida. It was later determined that oxygen canisters had been improperly stored on the plane. As the plane was climbing to its cruising altitude, the canisters exploded, sparked by a malfunction in the electrical system. Apparently, as a result of improper maintenance procedures and general operations, the fact that dangerous cargo was in the hold was not picked up. In contrast, TWA Flight 800 exploded mysteriously shortly after it took off from New York. In this case, apparently there were no faulty maintenance or operations procedures.

Upon review, every aspect of ValuJet's entire system was found to be seriously flawed. For instance, its maintenance operations were farmed out to the lowest bidder. In addition, the primary government oversight agency, the Federal Aviation Administration (FAA), failed to do its job.

The FAA was caught in a basic role conflict. On the one hand, it is the "cop" of the airline industry. It is concerned with policing the safety operations of the airlines. On the other hand, it is also the prime promoter of the airline industry. That is, it is a major "seller" of air travel.

It was later determined that both of these factors played an important role in the crash of the ValuJet plane. On the one hand, the FAA knew that ValuJet had one of the poorest safety records of any airline. On the other hand, it did not intervene seriously and quickly enough because of the FAA's desire to "promote and sell air travel."

TWA Flight 800 was an entirely different matter. In this case, *each* of the individual components of the overall system functioned well. What was lacking was the overall coordination between the various parts so that together they constituted a well-functioning *system*. For instance, TWA's fleet of 25-year-old aircraft was well maintained. Thus, the fault did not lie with TWA's aircraft or its maintenance procedures. In addition, if we assume that the FBI, the FAA, and the other government agencies that were involved performed their assigned functions well, then the fault did not lay with them.

What was lacking was the overall integration between each of these agencies so that they constituted a well-integrated system. For instance, during the course of the long investigation, it was learned that just six weeks prior to the TWA accident, one of the government agencies had simulated a terrorist bomb incident on the plane. This was learned when the FBI analyzed chemical residues found on the plane. However, because of the difficulties in passing information across government bureaucracies, this information was delayed for over six weeks from getting from one agency to the others involved in the overall investigation. This delay heightened the suspicions that the tragedy was caused by terrorism when apparently it was not.

Time and again, when one examines the causes of large-scale systems accidents, one finds that we are managing complex *systems* with a Machine Age mentality. Although we are clearly in a world where everything interacts with everything else, we persist in the belief that all complex systems can be broken apart into their separate components. Furthermore, we also believe that the components exist and function independently of the whole system of which they are a part. This is directly akin to arguing that a car would still be a car without a carburetor or a steering wheel. In addition, it is to kid ourselves into believing that a car's motion is due entirely to one and only one of its major parts, e.g., the wheels. Instead, the motion of a car is a function or a property of the whole system, i.e., the entire car. For another, it is to kid ourselves into believing that a modern car could function without an onboard computer that constantly monitors and regulates each of the complex systems that constitute the vehicle. These range from the systems that operate the hydraulic brakes to the exact mix of gasoline that is burned in the engine.

While the invention of the atomic bomb thrust us firmly into the Systems Age, we still insist in designing and operating complex systems with a pre-nuclear mentality. If we fail to change this way of thinking, then more and more large-scale crises will occur. We have no choice but to alter the fundamental ways in which we think about the world.

Both cases demonstrate the differences between conventional and critical thinking. In conventional thinking, the overall system will be taken care of if each of the parts is designed and functions well. In contrast, critical thinking insists that a system is always more than, or less than, the sum of its individual parts.[3] (If something is equal to the sum of its parts, then by definition it is not a "system.") The fact that each of the individual parts is designed well and performing well does not ensure that the overall system will work well. "Critical thinking" is "critical" precisely because it challenges the assumption that a complex system can be reduced to its component parts.

Connecting the Dots: The Ability to See the Big Picture, the Whole System

In the over 20 years that my colleagues and I have worked with senior executives to help them and their organizations prepare for crises, we have come across only *one individual* who, without our first prompting him, produced a "Big Picture" or systemic overview of his organization. This particular executive worked for one of the world's largest oil companies. In fact, it was one of OPEC's most important members.

In the course of performing a crisis audit, we asked this particular executive to talk about the crises that could affect his organization. He responded as follows:

> Consider the effects that plummeting world prices for oil would have on our organization. They would not only be numerous, but drastic.
>
> First of all, because of lower profits, we would have to lay off substantial numbers of our employees. This would directly affect the maintenance of our plants and facilities. There is no question that by itself this would lead to major accidents and other potentially catastrophic crises.
>
> In addition, laying off employees would certainly anger the unions. This anger would very likely spill over to worker malcontent. In turn, this could lead to a rise in workplace violence and sabotage. The increase in sabotage would further damage the production capacity of our refineries, leading to further lowered capacity, which in turn would deepen the economic crisis.
>
> Now you see why it is extremely easy to get caught and trapped in a vicious circle. However, by seeing all of these crises as an interacting system, it gives us the ability to anticipate them.
>
> Look at the matter this way. In the oil business, we commonly use the terms "upstream" and "downstream" activities. Upstream activities refer to all the events *leading to* the discovery of oil. Downstream activities refer to the processes involved in the *conversion* of oil into gasoline and other products.
>
> You have to look at the big picture when you're looking at all the crises that can affect you. You have to look at both the "upstream" and the "downstream" activities.
>
> If you can do this, then you are better able to anticipate what would serve as potential early warning signals that any of the crises in this complex pattern were about to occur. This allows you to think ahead and to reason as follows, "Well, if this happens *and* this happens, then what can I do to prevent it from setting off an uncontrolled chain reaction of other crises that will eventually destroy the organization?"

By "connecting the dots," this executive was able to think not only about preparing for each individual crisis, but also about how each individual crisis could set off an uncontrolled chain reaction of other crises. In this way, he could prepare for a *total system* of mutually occurring and interacting crises.

Emergency Response Is No Longer Sufficient

The events of September 11, 2001, exposed as never before the serious weaknesses of the United States' public and private systems. We are not anywhere near as prepared as we need to be in order to handle crises of that magnitude.

Certainly, the brave and dedicated firefighters and police officers of New York City and Washington demonstrated unequivocally that we are capable of responding exceedingly well to crises after they have occurred. However, we are nowhere near as good at anticipating them. While we may have excellent *emergency response* systems, we do not have nearly the same level of *crisis anticipation* systems.

How could we possibly have been prepared to pick up the early warning signals of a terrorist attack when the information was spread across 13 to 40 government agencies, depending how one "counts" them? The answer, of course, is that we can't. Anyone who has ever worked in an organization knows all too well the difficulties of communicating *within* a single bureaucracy. Imagine then the innumerable difficulties in communicating *across* different bureaucracies.

In many communities, there is not nearly the number of hospital beds that would be needed were a major bioterrorism attack to occur. We do not have anywhere near the amount of vaccines that would be required to treat a public health calamity.

CONCLUDING REMARKS: THE NEED FOR THINKING ABOUT THE UNTHINKABLE

The need for preparing for crises has never been greater. The need to prepare for the unthinkable has never been greater either.

By definition, the "unthinkable" is that which humans are unable to consider or imagine. In other words, the "unthinkable" is an extremely low probability but high consequence event. It is precisely the kind of crises that are overlooked by traditional Risk Management.

This book challenges the contention that humans are unable to consider or to imagine the unthinkable. While it is certainly impossible to have perfect knowledge of the unthinkable, for then it would clearly not be unthinkable, I wish to show that there are methods that can allow us to think about it more comprehensively and more systematically.

EXERCISES

1. Describe a typical application of Risk Management. That is, if you were a risk analyst for a major corporation, describe how you would proceed in advising

your organization which risks or potential crises it needs to prepare for and which ones it should neglect.

2. Explain how Risk Management would lead one to neglect crises such as those that occurred on 9/11. That is, what elements in performing a Risk Management analysis would lead one to neglect certain types of crises?

3. Describe as many differences as you can between Crisis Management and Crisis Leadership. Why do you think that at best most organizations practice Crisis Management and not Crisis Leadership? (Hint: Think of the differences between how Crisis Management and Crisis Leadership would treat a complex system. That is, which one would be most likely to treat the system as a "system"? In contrast, which field would most likely to break a system apart into its individual components and treat the components as self-standing entities?)

4. What is critical thinking and why is it central to Crisis Leadership?

5. List as many "unthinkable events" as you can. Describe the differences between how Risk Management, Crisis Management, and Crisis Leadership would approach each of these "unthinkables." Would each of them have a different approach to "thinking about the unthinkable"? Why?

6. Why do you think most senior executives are unable to see the Big Picture, i.e., to "connect the dots"?

7. Take any current crisis and produce a systems map of it. Like the single executive who was described in this chapter, make a diagram that shows how all the individual sub-crises are part of the bigger crisis.

NOTES

1. Fischhoff, B., "Risk Perception and Communication Unplugged: Twenty Years of Process," *Risk Analysis,* 1995, 15, 137–145; Fischhoff, B., "Acceptable Risk: A Conceptual Proposal," *Risk: Health, Safety and Environment,* 1994, 1, 1–28; Fischhoff, B., "Managing Risk Perceptions," *Issues in Science and Technology,* 1985, 2, 83–96; Fischhoff, B., Slovic, P., and Lichtenstein, S., "Knowing What You Want: Measuring Labile Values," in T. Wallsten (ed.), *Cognitive Processes in Choice and Decision Behavior,* Hillsdale, NJ: Lawrence Erlbaum, 1980, pp. 117–141.

2. Multiplying the percentage of a business or a product times its consequences is another way of performing Risk Management. In this form of Risk Management, one substitutes the percentage of a business for the probability of the occurrence of a particular crisis.

3. See Ackoff, Russell, *The Democratic Corporation: A Radical Prescription for Recreating Corporate America and Rediscovering Success,* New York: Oxford University Press, 1994.

CHAPTER 3

THE FAILURE
OF CONVENTIONAL
ORGANIZATIONS

*Even when America sets its own agenda, there are serious prob-
lems. The U.S. spends more than 90 percent of its $35 billion
annual intelligence budget on spying gadgetry rather than on gath-
ering human intelligence, and most of that money goes not to the
C.I.A. but to spy agencies within the Department of Defense, such
as the National Security Agency (which does eavesdropping and
code-breaking) and the National Reconnaissance Office (which
flies imagery satellites). The priciest gadgets are not always the
ones suited to fighting the terrorist threat...*

*High-tech surveillance can do little to track adversaries like
the Sept. 11 hijackers, especially if they are in the U.S. legally and
careful about what they say on the phone. So why does the C.I.A.
persist in spying the wrong way? Part of the answer lies in the culture of secrecy that arose during the Cold War and continues to rule
the agency's heart and mind.*

Source: Massimo Calabresi and Romesh Ratnesar, "Can We Stop the Next Attack?"
TIME, March 11, 2002, 28–29.

The previous chapter examined the failures of conventional thinking and its impact
on Crisis Management. This chapter examines how the basic design of institutions,
established in the early twentieth century, is greatly responsible for the inability of
today's organizations to respond to crises.

THE DESIGN OF GM

In 1963, the seminal business autobiography of one of General Motor's (GM) first
CEOs, Alfred P. Sloan, Jr., *My Years with General Motors,*[1] was published. It still is
one of the most important books in the short history of Crisis Management.

While it became an instant bestseller—it was one of the first "business block-
busters"—it was never recognized nor referred to as a book on Crisis Management.
Although the word "crisis" occurs repeatedly throughout Sloan's text, the term

nevertheless was not listed in the index. Undoubtedly this was due to the fact that it was not until 19 years later that the modern field of Crisis Management was invented. The 1982 poisonings involving Tylenol capsules in a suburb of Chicago are generally recognized as the starting point of the modern field of Crisis Management.[2]

Sloan's autobiography makes perfectly clear that, although it has undergone numerous modifications, the design of GM that emerged in the 1920s remains essentially unchanged. Furthermore, since Sloan's design was adopted widely by American businesses and government agencies, it still applies to them as well. Most important, since this design was the direct response to the particular set of crises that GM faced in the 1920s, *today's organizations are largely the result of the response to the crises of 80 years ago!* No wonder that our organizations respond poorly to contemporary crises such as sexual harassment, workplace violence, and terrorism. In short, today's organizations are responding to crises for which they were not designed. In effect, the design of today's organizations has been frozen in time.

Notice that I am not saying that organizations have not changed substantially over the course of the twentieth century and the early twenty-first. They have. But despite all the appearance of change, their underlying operations and design, and even more the mentality on which they are based, are essentially the same as in the nineteenth and early twentieth centuries. Today's organizations are still rooted in Machine Age thinking.

GM'S FOUR MAJOR CRISES

In the late 1910s and early 1920s, GM faced four crises:

1. Extreme ups and downs in the general economy (what else is new!);
2. Gaining control over its huge inventory of cars—believe it or not, GM didn't know how many cars it was producing annually;
3. Getting accurate and timely sales data from GM's dealers (GM didn't know how many cars it was actually selling); and
4. Getting the various car divisions to share their revenues with the central corporation on a continuing basis.

Unlike far too many of today's CEOs, Sloan did not opt for short-term, Band-Aid solutions. He and his colleagues fashioned and pushed through permanent changes in the overall operating structure of GM. The most important was the creation of the Finance Committee at the very top of the corporation.

While Sloan did not invent *the field* or *the discipline* of Finance, he did establish the world's first Finance Department. This fact alone justifies a brief history of Crisis Management. (This brief history is continued in the next chapter.) Far too many people assume—quite erroneously—that Finance Departments have been around since time immemorial.

The job of the Finance Committee was twofold: first, to get an accurate picture of the corporation's total revenues and expenses, and more important, to foster long-term economic planning so that the corporation could gain as much control as was possible over its financial destiny. That this structure worked so well is one of the reasons why GM became, and until relatively recently was, the world's largest corporation. (In the 1960s, GM had 50 percent of the world car market. By the end of the late 1990s, this had shrunk to 25 percent, an "unthinkable" crisis.)

The distinctive quality of Sloan's attitude and responses cannot be overemphasized. Even though the fluctuations and the downturns in the general economy were temporary, Sloan was not shortsighted. He did not engage in the rationalizations that far too many of today's executives use after a crisis has passed: "Whew, that's over! Let's put it behind us and get back to 'business as usual.' Let's not wallow in what's depressing."

Of course, it can be argued that without adequate financial controls there would be no corporation at all. By definition, anything that threatens a corporation's financial base will be a concern of the first order. It will call for drastic, and even permanent, solutions. A financial crisis of any kind will automatically receive and command the attention it deserves.

While this may be true, it is also a fact that today's crises pose challenges that Sloan and his colleagues could never have envisioned. Indeed, today's crises have the potential to wreak extreme financial havoc (e.g., the Ford/Firestone debacle, Enron), and in some cases, destroy the very existence of a corporation (e.g., the businesses that were housed in the World Trade Center). (As this book is written, there is the real possibility that Enron auditor Arthur Andersen will go out of existence.) The $64 billion questions thus become: "What *will* it take for today's organizations to realize that they need to change their basic operating structures so that they can respond effectively to crises far beyond those ever experienced and envisioned by Sloan and his colleagues?" and "What new operating structures *are* required if today's organizations are to respond effectively to the crises they face?"[3]

THE NEED FOR CRISIS LEADERSHIP

The preceding questions are among the most important that this book addresses. However, in addition to answering them, we believe that something even more fundamental is required. As it has been developed and practiced over the past 20 years, Crisis Management is no longer adequate. As I argued in Chapter Two, an entirely new concept, Crisis Leadership, is required.

Although Sloan didn't use the term "infrastructure," he did in fact put into place a deliberate structure for managing crises. The importance of this is best seen by means of the following: If today we were to walk into any corporation and inquire whether it had a department specifically dedicated to Finance, we would be met with looks of extreme bewilderment. The very question would be enough to certify that one was "unbalanced." However, if we were to walk into the same corporation and inquire whether there was a dedicated infrastructure for Crisis Leadership, we would be met with looks of bewilderment and confusion. The two "looks" would not be the same.

An organization would be considered crazy if it did *not* have a Finance Department as well as a senior executive for Finance. In the case of Crisis Leadership, however, we would be considered crazy if we merely thought that such a department was necessary!

Far too many executives believe that adding a specific infrastructure for Crisis Leadership is tantamount to adding another layer of bureaucracy. This is not the case. Not all structures are the same. They are not all inherently bad.

There is all the difference in the world between structures that *enable* and those that *stifle* and strangle an organization. Enabling structures are not the same as bureaucratic ones.[4] I am not thereby calling for adding bureaucratic layers to an organization. Instead, I am calling for the addition of *appropriate* structures that will allow global corporations to give proper autonomy to local operating units. This is because local units know their local markets better than some bureaucrat who is ensconced at headquarters. Yet, global corporations must still have the appropriate machinery for responding to crises that affect the whole of an organization.

The source of the difficulty lies in confusing an *integrated* design that is critical to Crisis Leadership with one that is *centralized* and *bureaucratic* which is typical of Crisis Management. As we shall see, "integration" is not the same as a "primitive fusion" of business functions.

There is no getting around the fact that today's organizations are global, period. This means that a crisis in one locale can swiftly escalate into a crisis for an entire organization. Therefore, both globally integrated and locally responsible structures are needed.[5]

AN EXAMPLE: THE COCA-COLA COMPANY'S "BELGIUM CRISIS"

A perfect example is the "Belgium crisis" that the Coca-Cola Company experienced a few years ago. Briefly, Belgian health authorities were receiving mounting complaints that children were becoming sick after drinking Coca-Cola. The complaints were to the effect that the cans and the drink smelled and tasted "funny." The Coca-Cola Company dismissed the complaints as "merely psychological."

Technical analyses revealed that in fact there was nothing wrong with the quality of the products. Therefore, the "problem" had to be in the minds of consumers. By the time that the Coca-Cola executives realized that no amount of technical information or "gobbledygook" was going to persuade consumers to stop feeling sick, they had a full-blown crisis on their hands. In addition, the Belgian minister of Health became so infuriated at Coca-Cola's delayed response to the crisis that he ordered that all cans of Coca-Cola be pulled from the shelves of all of the stores throughout Belgium.

The crisis did not stop there. In order to distance themselves as much from the crisis, McDonald's, one of Coca-Cola's largest partners, stopped serving Coke in all of its outlets.

As a result of his poor handling of the crisis, the CEO of Coca-Cola, M. Douglas Ivester, was fired. This was not enough to stave off the damage done to Coca-Cola's reputation worldwide.

THE CHIEF CRISIS OFFICER

Because Finance Departments have been around for 80 years, we tend to believe that a formalized financial function has always been present. However, if we were able to transport ourselves back in time to when Sloan was CEO of GM, we would realize that his proposals for meeting the crises of his times were no less radical than ours.

If today's organizations are to respond effectively to crises, then they will need a chief crisis officer. There is no longer any excuse for every organization's *not* having a full-time, senior executive in charge of examining, and improving upon, the crisis capabilities of his or her organization.

Organizations need something even more radical. They need world-class Crisis Learning and Signal Detection Centers. Among the major purposes of such centers are the constant monitoring of early warning signals from around the globe announcing the occurrence of potential crises and unthinkables. Of course, this cannot be accomplished with any guarantee of perfection. This does not relieve us from the responsibility of doing everything humanly possible to prevent crises. To borrow an analogy from the field of medicine, the fact that we cannot treat perfectly each of the innumerable factors responsible for heart disease does not relieve us from the responsibility of attacking each of them as aggressively as we can.

A major function of such Crisis Learning Centers is to study the patterns associated with past crises, to distill the critical lessons from these patterns, and to ensure that the organization puts these lessons into practice so that the potential for future crises is lowered considerably. Understanding these patterns involves learning when, where, and why crises have occurred, and what could have lowered the chances of their occurrence, as well as their impacts. Although it is clearly impossible to prevent all crises, being prepared for *any* crisis speeds up substantially one's recovery time. Being prepared also dramatically lowers the economic costs of a particular crisis. It lessens the psychological impacts as well.

MOVING CRISIS LEADERSHIP TO THE CENTER

We cannot expect to win new wars with old tactics. Crisis Leadership has to move from the *periphery* of organizations to their center. This means that *all organizations need to be redesigned around Crisis Leadership.* A key element of this new design is the Crisis Learning Center.

FAULTY ASSUMPTIONS

Our brief examination of the history of the design of the American corporation has revealed that they have been built on two powerful but faulty assumptions:

- An organization *is* a machine; i.e., it can be broken apart into separate departments, functions, and divisions. In short, it is nothing more than the sum of self-standing and isolated silos.

- As new problems and issues arise, new departments, functions, and silos can be added to the basic design without disturbing it in any essential way.[6]

Both of these assumptions are wrong, dead wrong!

CONCLUDING REMARKS: FLAWED BY DESIGN

In *Flawed by Design*,[7] UCLA political scientist Amy Zegart has argued convincingly that government agencies have fared no better than private corporations when it comes to managing crises. Zegart has shown why the agencies charged with monitoring terrorist and intelligence information for the U.S. government were flawed from their inception, i.e., by deliberate design. The CIA, FBI, and FAA were "deliberately designed" *not* to share information in a timely and efficient fashion.

This was not done out of malicious intent. It was done out of the understandable fears that the concentration of terrorism information in a single agency would lead inevitably to abuses of power by the U.S. government. It was also the result of political in-fighting between the House of Representatives, the Senate, the president, and the branches of the armed forces over the control of information with regard to terrorism. In short, the fight was over who would have control over what. The result is a complete mishmash of agencies charged with collecting, analyzing, and disseminating intelligence information to the right governmental units and persons so that timely action can be taken. Most critical of all, the design basically no longer works. As a consequence, Zegart argues convincingly, basic agencies have to be fundamentally redesigned that that they can function in an integrated manner. They certainly do *not* need to be fused into a single, central, bumbling, bureaucratic agency.

EXERCISES

1. Trace the historical forces that have led to the design of today's institutions. Why are these designs no longer adequate for Crisis Leadership?
2. Outline some of the new features that today's organizations must have in order to respond to crises more effectively.
3. Outline in more detail the job function/description of a chief crisis officer.

NOTES

1. Sloan, Alfred P., Jr., *My Years With General Motors,* New York: Currency Doubleday, 1963.
2. See Mitroff, Ian I., and Anagnos, G. (2000), *Managing Crises Before They Happen: What Every Executive and Manager Needs to Know about Crisis Management,* New York: AMACOM. See also Pauchant, Thierry C., and Mitroff, Ian I., *Transforming the Crisis-Prone Organization: Preventing Individual, Organizational, and Environmental Tragedies,* San Francisco: Jossey-Bass, 1992.
3. See Adler, P.S., and Borys, B., "Two Types of Bureaucracy: Enabling and Coercive," *Administrative Science Quarterly,* 1996, 41: 61–89; Ralph H. Kilmann, *Quantum Organizations: A*

New Paradigm for Achieving Organizational Success and Personal Meaning, Palo Alto, CA: Consulting Psychologists Press/Davies-Black, 2001. See also Weick, Karl E., Sutcliffe, Kathleen M., and Quinn, Robert E., *Managing the Unexpected: Assuring High Performance in an Age of Complexity,* San Francisco: Jossey-Bass, 2001.

4.   See Kilmann, op. cit.

5.   Bartlett, C.A., and Ghoshal, S., "Beyond the M-form: Toward a Managerial Theory of the Firm, *Strategic Management Journal,* 1993, 14(special issue): 23–46; Bartlett, C.A. and Ghoshal, S., "Managing Across Borders: New Strategic Requirements," *Sloan Management Review,* 1987, 7–17.

6.   Taylor, F.W., *The Principles of Scientific Management,* New York: Norton, 1967; Thompson, J., *Organizations in Action: Social Science Bases of Administrative Theory,* New York: McGraw-Hill, 1967.

7.   Zegart, Amy B., *Flawed by Design: The Evolution of the CIA, JCS and NSC,* Stanford, CA: Stanford University Press, 1999.

CHAPTER *4*

THE FAILURE OF CONVENTIONAL RESPONSES

After a decade of litigating S.U.V. rollovers [lawyer Tab] Turner has amassed an extraordinary library of Ford internal documents, and he e-mails them around the nation with gusto, to reporters, Congressional investigators, Nader types, and fellow plaintiff attorneys. Throughout the summer and fall, he supplied crucial documents to reporters as they vied to be the first to figure out who knew what when *at Ford and Firestone concerning defective tires that federal investigators have now linked to 148 deaths, mainly in Explorers.*

...Turner ...provided the Ford documents showing that when the Explorer was developed in the late 1980's, the prototype repeatedly failed Ford's own roll over tests; and ...Turner ...provided documents showing that Ford played a major role in developing the flawed Firestone tire.

Source: Michael Winerip, "What's Tab Turner Got Against Ford?" *New York Times Magazine,* December 17, 2000, 48–49.

For the past 20 years, my colleagues and I have studied and consulted with regard to hundreds of crises. They span every imaginable type.

As a result of our studies, we believe that we have discerned a general pattern. This pattern indicates in no uncertain terms that crises don't just happen. Indeed, as we shall see in the next chapter, Charles Perrow has argued persuasively that many crises are "built into" the complex systems we have created.[1] They are, in fact, integral aspects of the Systems Age. They would not have been possible in the relative simplicity of the Machine Age, i.e., the period following the Industrial Revolution.

This chapter discusses the interactions between the characteristics of crises and the largely inappropriate responses of top executives and organizations. As we shall see, the interactions make the initial crisis, or crises, even worse.

THREE CRISES REVEAL THE PATTERN

Three crises in particular illustrate the point: the crash of the ValuJet airliner in 1996, the Firestone/Ford tire crisis in August 2000, and the World Trade Center and

Pentagon disasters of September 11, 2001 (9/11). The fact that these three crises are so different illustrates that beneath the surface, there is a pattern. (As this book was being written, the crises in the Roman Catholic church, Enron, and Worldcom were unfolding. These also fit the general pattern.)

The criteria for selecting these crises are not random. For one, all of them received extensive media coverage. In fact, the coverage went on for weeks and even months. As a result, there were ample opportunities to examine how each crisis developed over time, how each played out in the media, and how the various organizations involved responded. In addition, the coverage was extensive not only on television but in the print media as well. Finally, there was extensive coverage of virtually every aspect of how the organizations handled the crises. Thus, I was able to examine what they did well, and did not do well, at every stage of their unfolding.

Each crisis involved serious injuries and deaths. In the case of ValuJet, all 110 people on board died upon impact of an airliner in a Florida swamp. In the case of the Firestone/Ford tire crisis, approximately 150 people have died (this number continues to grow despite the extensive recall) and hundreds more were seriously injured as the result of tire blowouts on Ford Explorers. In the case of the World Trade Center and Pentagon attacks, at the current time, the number of dead has been estimated at 3,063. As we shall see shortly, this uncertainty with regard to the casualty count is one of the worst, and most prominent, features of crises.

The differences between them are just as important. ValuJet's crisis involved a particularly gruesome form of death, the crash of an airplane. While death was presumed to be immediate, the remains were difficult to recover given the heat, the humidity, the depth of the swamp, and the toxic chemicals that seeped from the airplane, plus the presence of alligators. The difficult recovery added an extra emotional layer to the crisis.

Firestone/Ford, on the other hand, possesses critical features that airline crashes do not. First of all, no matter how common air travel has become, one does not crash into a Florida swamp every day. On the other hand, nearly everyone drives or rides in a vehicle every day. Driving on tires is thus much more widespread. Finally, ValuJet involves a service while Firestone/Ford involves a consumer product. Thus, the crises "cover" or "span" different types of businesses. While it is likely that more people can relate directly to Firestone/Ford than they can to ValuJet, each case represents one end of the spectrum. The World Trade Center and Pentagon, however, involved deliberate acts of terrorism, which ValuJet and Ford/Firestone do not.

To elicit the general pattern, I performed the same set of detailed operations. First, for as long as each crisis was featured prominently in the daily news, I taped as much of the daily coverage as possible. Next, every few days, I selected three to five video segments that captured its ongoing major developments. In this way, I boiled nine to 12 weeks of coverage for each crisis down to an hour and a half.

THE COMMON PATTERN: KEY ELEMENTS

The following elements constitute the general pattern. Recognizing and responding well to each is central to the exercise of Crisis Leadership.

Improper leadership with respect to any of the elements not only causes one to mismanage the specific crisis at hand, but it also sets off a chain reaction of additional crises. Organizations that do poorly on Crisis Leadership mishandle each of the following key elements. If the initial crises aren't bad enough, then how an organization responds subsequently is likely to make it even worse.

Tremendous Ethical and Technical Uncertainty

From the earliest stages of a crisis, there is tremendous uncertainty as to its exact nature, detailed causes, and even its exact type.[2] As strange as it may sound, it is not known for sure what the crisis or crises are. To be sure, the "surface or presenting crisis" seems apparent, i.e., the crash or the explosion of a plane, the failure of tires, or terrorist actions, but the full set of the underlying *causes, reasons, or factors that are responsible* for the crisis are not known. In addition, one does not know for sure that other crises that will inevitably follow if the current crisis is handled improperly. Furthermore, it is not known how other critical factors, such as all of the stakeholders or key players, will "rise to the surface" in response to how the initial crisis is handled.[3]

As a result, there is tremendous technical and ethical uncertainty regarding what one should do, especially with respect to how much responsibility one should assume from the beginning. In fact, the more horrendous the crisis, the more that certainty will be lacking. Considerable uncertainty is an integral feature of all crises, yet there is an intense need for certainty. This lack of certainty intensifies the anxiety that is an integral part of the crisis.

There is also tremendous uncertainty regarding the proper assumptions that one has to make with regard to all the "unknowns." Thus, the actions that one should take are also highly uncertain. In spite of this, or because of it, one has to assume ethical and moral leadership from the very beginning if one is to capture and hold the ethical/moral "high ground." This of course raises the critical question, "How does one lead, not manage, the ethical and the technical uncertainty that is an essential aspect of all crises?" One cannot delay actions for too long because such delays will not only add to the crisis, but set off new ones as well.

New York Mayor Rudolph Giuliani is perhaps the role model for how to lead in times of crisis. First and foremost, he was available. He showed up everywhere all of the time. When he didn't know something, he said that he didn't know. He didn't vacillate. He also exhibited deep and sincere emotional concern. In this way, he was not distant from the crisis in any way.

Moral Trial by Compelling Images

The same graphic images, including scenes of death, destruction, and injuries, are shown over and over again. Each replay is a "self-contained moral story" so that the viewer does not have to refer to any early images or stories in order to get the point of the tragedy.

Each scene is also a self-contained moral story in that there are clear "victims" and "villains." The identities of the victims and the villains are locked in early in the unfolding crisis and tend to become permanent. In this way, the media removes any traces of moral ambiguity.

Referring back to the first point, certainty and uncertainty exist side by side. On the one hand, there is technical uncertainty regarding the causes of a crisis and therefore there is uncertainly regarding what one should do ethically and technically to alleviate it. On the other hand, the media attempt to establish moral certainty by locking in the victims versus villains. In fact, the media attempt to create moral certainty both consciously and unconsciously in order to soothe the underlying emotions and anxieties of the public.

This does not mean that the media are entirely to blame for whether an organization or an institution is perceived as a victim or a villain. Indeed, as we shall see, a substantial part of the blame rests on the organizations and institutions themselves.

In short, the same statistics of product-related deaths and injuries are repeated ad nauseam. The same scenes of planes crashing into buildings are replayed endlessly.

As a result, the images have a narcotic-like effect, mesmerizing the audience. They are extremely compelling from a moral and emotional standpoint. Their fundamental point is to grip the audience, not inform it.

Objectivity Is a Turnoff

Public and private institutions involved in crises attempt to use *objective* numbers and statistics to defend themselves and to get the public to perceive the situation from their standpoint. This only confirms the public's perception of the organizations as the villains.

On the other hand, the media use intensely *personal* numbers and statistics to connect emotionally and to side with the public against the organizations.[4] The media present the individual faces of personal tragedies, "people just like you and me." In the case of the World Trade Center, they focus in on individual acts of heroism. The result is the message: "That could be you and me." The message is also: "We, the media, are on your side against the big, bad organizations whether they be private companies or government agencies." The use of objective statistics and numbers is further interpreted by the media and the public as proof of guilt.

The Court of Public Opinion Versus the Court of Law

The media convict the organizations of high moral crimes and misdemeanors. While the legal system presumes one is innocent until proven guilty, the media reverse the procedure. The burden is on the organizations to prove their innocence. In short, the organization is presumed guilty until proven otherwise. The organizations are much more easily and quickly convicted in the "court of public opinion" than they are in the formal courts. Furthermore, the threshold for conviction is much lower in the court of public opinion than it is in the formal legal system. Once a person or an organization is perceived as a "villain," it is extremely difficult to shed the label.

The media use the "trappings" of the legal system to convict the institutions. For instance, early on in the Firestone/Ford crisis, the CNN legal program *Burden of Proof* featuring Roger Cossack and Greta Van Susteren devoted a whole episode to Firestone/Ford. Several lawyers and a tire expert were interviewed. One of the lawyers was engaged in bringing lawsuits against both Ford and Firestone. While Susteren said repeatedly that "all of the data are not in" and that "hence, we cannot convict either company," the intent was just the same. The companies were still "convicted in absentia."

Chain Reaction

The statements given by executives and officials are often too late to overcome the media's negative stories and the perceptions that have been fostered. Furthermore, the statements are almost always immediately contradicted by "unfolding information" that the media quickly surface. As a result, the organizations fall deeper and deeper into new and even worse crises. In slightly different words, a chain reaction of further crises ensues.

No Secrets/Complete Transparency

The media use eye-catching graphics to "blow up" intercompany and interagency reports to further convict them in the court of public opinion. The media also use graphics to explain difficult, complex, and arcane technical subjects such as the intricacies of tire production. In fact, they do this much better than do the organizations, such as Firestone. While the organizations may be "better technical experts," the media excel at reducing complex subjects to easily grasped terms.

In the case of the World Trade Center, several of the major networks used polished animations to illustrate what happens when a plane crashes into a tall building and the structural steel is heated to a temperature where it can no longer support the building's weight.

Whether the media make technical subjects overly simplistic is not the main point. Whether correct or not, the effect is that every aspect of an organization becomes completely transparent. In today's media-saturated world, there are no longer any secrets about a person, company, organization, or institution. The media can find out anything they want about anybody or any organization and institution. For instance:

> … from 1995 to 1997, Goodyear had a contract to produce about half the tires for the Explorer; those 2.6 million Goodyears were inflated to a 26 p.s.i. and did not fail the way Firestones did.
>
> The explanation for that may be the obvious—Goodyear produced a better tire, which had more of a safety margin to absorb the stress of 26 p.s.i. Tread separations have not been a problem on Explorers with Goodyear Wranglers.
>
> So why didn't Ford stay with the superior Goodyear for its Explorers? Money. In 1996, Goodyear decided it couldn't produce an Explorer tire at the price Ford was willing to pay.
>
> …at the time Ford thought it was getting a comparable quality tire from Firestone at "better value. In retrospect, we were wrong."[5]

Widening of the Crisis(es)

The three crises widen not only to other members of the same industry, but also to the government agencies charged with overseeing the industry. In the case of ValuJet, the FAA was implicated; in the case of Firestone/Ford, it was the National Highway Transportation Safety Administration. In the case of the World Trade Center and the Pentagon, more than 40 agencies were involved in monitoring potential acts of terrorism. The fact that these agencies failed to get timely information across their bureaucracies became a part of the central crisis.

Things that otherwise would have been below the threshold of news rose to the surface, such as recalls of other Ford products. Airline crashes that occurred soon after the World Trade Center bombings also received considerable attention

In each case, it is argued convincingly that the government oversight agencies failed to do their jobs. In many cases, this is due to the lack of funding by the Congress and/or political ideology that favors "small government." For instance, consider the following:

> Is sudden acceleration real? Or are some S.U.V.s dangerously prone to roll over? What is an acceptable tire-tread failure rate? There would be no need for [lawyers such as] Tab Turners if a trusted referee existed to arbitrate the claims of auto companies, Nader groups, insurers, and motorists. Unfortunately, the federal body set up to do so, N.H.T.S.A., is understaffed, slow to react, unreliable, and the captive of all sort of political agendas. The last time N.H.T.S.A. was aggressive was under Jimmy Carter. Spurred by an eerily similar tire failure—the recall of millions of Firestone 500 radials—[Jill] Claybrook [director of N.H.T.S.A. under Carter] recommended tough new standards for tires and light trucks that would have affected the first generation of S.U.V.'s. And then came Ronald Reagan. Reagan slashed the agency's budget, revoking several new regulations—including a dashboard warning light for tire-inflation problems.
>
> ... If there were an auto defect, a N.H.T.S.A. administrator might well be among the last Americans to know.[6]

Criminalization

As a result of the "outrageous behavior" of organizations and institutions, such as the failure to heed early warning signals and to respond promptly and appropriately, Congress and state legislatures threaten to pass tougher "criminal laws" against "irresponsible and criminal executive behavior." The heads of major agencies are castigated before Congress.

Everything Potentially Becomes Major

The laser-like focus of the media is turned on all company operations, turning minor incidents such as product recalls that would never have received attention into additional and potentially major crises.

The Blame Game

If multiple companies and organizations are involved, and they usually are, they engage in a game of blaming one another and even the consumer for the problems. For example, Ford and Firestone blamed each other, as well as consumers, for the improper inflation of tires.

Enron is a case in point. There was not only internal blame, i.e., those who blew the whistle against top Enron officials, but there was also considerable blaming between Enron and its auditor, Arthur Andersen. As a result, all parties, save the whistle-blowers, were damaged seriously.

Early Warning Signals

Early warning signals from other agencies, companies, countries, and industries are ignored or discounted and "explained away." In the case of Firestone/Ford, it was argued by both companies that problems in Venezuela and Saudi Arabia did not apply to the United States because U.S. operating conditions were very different. U.S. trucks and tires do not operate in the same high temperature and humidity conditions, so the data were deemed irrelevant.

Lessons Ignored, Not Learned

The lessons from previous crises not only are displayed prominently by the media, but it is shown that those lessons have been ignored. For example, after the crashes of ValuJet's airliner and TWA Flight 800, it was revealed that the FAA failed to implement changes that would have picked up the intrusion of terrorism into the airline industry. The TV program *60 Minutes* featured several segments with retired FAA inspectors who discussed in detail how easy it is to carry guns, knives, and bombs past airport security systems. In this way, the entire system is judged to be a failure.

The organizations' failure to learn is used as a scorecard to further judge irresponsible behavior. Most damaging of all, the scorecard directly contradicts the contention that the present crisis is an aberration. For instance, out of the ten largest tire recalls in U.S. history, Firestone has been involved in five. The media thus conclude that it is the same old pattern of not learning from past crises. As a result, the contention that the present crisis is merely an aberration is demolished.

Abandon the Ship

Dealers and other key stakeholders abandon the organizations in an attempt to save themselves. For instance, if it would help them to sell Ford Explorers, then Ford dealers were more than willing to switch to other tires. In fact, a number of dealers said that they would no longer use "Stone" tires of any kind. Not only would they not carry Firestone tires, but they also would not carry tires from Bridgestone, the parent company of Firestone.

A Company Is Forced to Hire an Independent Investigator

Repeated studies of crises show that an organization is extremely well advised to hire an independent investigator to either confirm or disconfirm the "facts of a crisis" as the organizations see them. Unless the company hires an independent investigator on its own, it will be forced to do so later. By that time, however, the company's credibility will have precariously shrunk. A company is well advised to get the "complete and awful truth" out as soon as possible when it still has a semblance of control and credibility.

Companies End Up Doing the Right Thing Too Late

Organizations almost always end up doing at the tail end of the crisis what they staunchly refused to do at the beginning! For instance, in the case of the Ford/Firestone tire crisis, Firestone finally made more replacement tires available when from the very beginning the company claimed that this was "impossible" to do.

Internal Contradictions

While this aspect is strongly related to point 5, (a Chain Reaction of further crises ensues because of internal contradictions that are revealed by the media.), there are subtle differences. When they finally appear, the statements of company or agency officials are almost always followed immediately by news clips showing internal company documents that directly contradict the statements. As a result, the credibility of the organizations plummets.

A company has to have a consistent story, and it has to be the "complete and full truth" no matter how bad it is. For this reason, I strongly advise an organization to get this truth out as soon as possible so as to minimize further damage. The longer that the "truth" dribbles out, the further one becomes entrenched into the role of a villain.

CONCLUDING REMARKS

If the unthinkable weren't bad enough in itself, how an organization responds to a crisis can make it even worse. It all depends fundamentally upon whether one recognizes the basic pattern that has been presented in this chapter, and either acts to reinforce it, or to break it. One thing is clear. In order to break a pattern, one must be aware of it.

EXERCISES

1. Show how a recent crisis fits the general pattern described in this chapter.
2. At every step of the crisis, show what the top executives of the organization and/or related government oversight agencies should have done to break the pattern.

NOTES

1. Perrow, Charles, *Normal Accidents: Living with High Risk Technologies,* New York: Basic Books, 1984.

2. Alexander, D., "Scenario Methodology for Teaching Principles of Emergency Management," *Disaster Prevention and Management,* 2000, 9(2): 89–97; Clair, J.A., "Turning Poison into Medicine: A Grounded Theoretical Analysis of Processes, Pathologies, and Designs in the Detection of Potential Organizations Crises," unpublished dissertation, University of Southern California, Los Angeles, 1993; Fink, S., "Crisis Management: Planning for the Inevitable," New York: American Management Association, 1986; Fischhoff, B., "Risk Perception and Communication Unplugged: Twenty Years of Process," *Risk Analysis,* 1995, 15, 137–145; Fischhoff, B., "Acceptable Risk: A Conceptual Proposal," *Risk: Health, Safety and Environment,* 1994, I, 1–28; Fischhoff, B., "Managing Risk Perceptions," *Issues in Science and Technology,* 1985, 2, 83–96; Fischhoff, B., Slovic, P., and Lichtenstein, S., "Knowing What You Want: Measuring Labile Values," in T. Wallsten (ed.), *Cognitive Processes in Choice and Decision Behavior,* Hillsdale, NJ: Lawrence Erlbaum, 1980, 117–141; Heath, R.L., and Gay, C.D., "Risk Communication: Involvement, Uncertainty, and Control's Effect on Information Scanning and Monitoring by Expert Stakeholders," *Management Communication Quarterly,* 1997, 10(3): 342–372; Keown-McMullan, C., "Crisis: When Does a Molehill Become a Mountain?" *Disaster Prevention and Management,* 1997, 6(1): 4–10; Kovoor, S., "Crisis Preparation in Technical Organizations: A Study Using a Multi-Dimensional Approach," unpublished dissertation, University of Southern California, Los Angeles, 1991; Lee, R.G., and Russo, R.J., "Dealing with Disasters Takes Careful Planning Ahead of Time," *Building Design and Construction,* 1996, 37(9): f37–8; March, J.G., and Shapira, J., "Managerial Perspectives on Risk and Risk Taking," *Management Science* (November 1987): 1404–1418; Mitroff, I I., and Anagnos, G., *Managing Crises Before They Happen: What Every Executive and Manager Needs to Know about Crisis Management,* New York: AMACOM, 2000; Mitroff, I.I., Pearson, C.M., and Harrington, L.K., *The Essential Guide to Managing Corporate Crises,* New York: Oxford University Press, 1996; Mitroff, I.I., and Pauchant, T.C., *We're So Big and Powerful Nothing Bad Can Happen to Us: An Investigation of America's Crisis Prone Corporations,* Secaucus, NJ: Carol Pub. Group, 1990; Mitroff, I., Pauchant, T., and Shrivastava, P., "The Structure of Man-Made Organization Crises," *Technological Forecasting and Social Change,* 1988, 33: 83–107; Mitroff, I. I., Shrivastava, P., and F. Udwadia, "Effective Crisis Management," *Academy of Management Executives,* 1987, 1(3): 283–292; Seeger, M.W., and Ulmer, R.R., "Virtuous Responses to Organizational Crises: Aaron Feuerstein and Milt Cole," *Journal of Business Ethics,* 2001, 31(4) 369–376; Shrivastava, P., and Mitroff, I., "Strategic Management of Corporate Crises," *Columbia Journal of World Business,* 1987, 22(1): 5–11; Smith, R., "Planning for Contingencies," *Industrial Management and Data Systems,* 1996, 96(6): 27–28; Starbuck, W., Greve, A., and Hedberg, B., "Responding to Crises," *Journal of Business Administration,* Spring, 1978 reprinted in J. Quinn and H. Mintzberg (eds., 1992), *The Strategy Process,* Englewood Cliffs, NJ: Prentice Hall, 1978; Staw, B.M., Sandelands, L.E., and Dutton, J.E., "Threat-Rigidity Effects in Organizational Behavior: A Multilevel

Analysis," *Administrative Science Quarterly*, 1981, 266(4): 501–525; Weick, K.E., and Sutcliffe, K.M., *Managing the Unexpected: Assuring High Performance in an Age of Complexity*, University of Michigan Business School Management Series, San Francisco: Jossey-Bass, 2001; Weick, K.E., "The Collapse of Sensemaking in Organizations: The Mann Gulch Disaster," *Administrative Science Quarterly*, 1993, 38, 628–652.

3.   See Mitroff, Ian I., and Linstone, Harold A., *The Unbounded Mind: Breaking the Chains of Traditional Business Thinking*, New York: Oxford University Press, 1993, for a detailed discussion of Stakeholder Analysis.

4.   For further, and contrasting, views on the role of the media in crises see Conn, W.D., Owens, W. L., and Rich, R.C., "Communicating with the Public about Hazardous Materials: An Examination of Local Practice," *EPA Report No. 230-04-90-077*, Blacksburg, VA: Virginia Polytechnic Institute & State University, University Center for Environmental & Hazardous Materials Studies, 1990; Covello, V. T., "Risk Communication: An Emerging Area of Health Communication," in S.A. Deetz (ed.), *Communication Yearbook 15* (pp. 359–373), Newbury Park, CA: Sage, 1992; Covello, V.T., Sandman, P.M., and Slovic, P., "Risk Communication, Risk Statistics and Risk Comparisons: A Manual for Plant Managers," Washington, DC: Chemical Manufacturers Association, 1988; Heath and Gay, op. cit.; Heath, R.L., "Corporate Issues Management: Theoretical Underpinnings and Research Foundations," in L.A. Grunig and J.E. Grunig (eds.), *Public Relations Research Annual*, Vol. 2, pp. 29–65, Hillsdale, NJ: Lawrence Erlbaum, 1990; Heath, R.L., and Nathan, K., "Public Relations' Role in Risk Communication: Information, Rhetoric and Power, *Public Relations Quarterly*, 1990: 15–22; Massey, J.E., "Managing Organization Legitimacy: Communication Strategies for Organizations In Crisis," *Journal of Business Communication*, April 2001, 38(2): 153–183; Skerlep, Andrej, "Re-Evaluating the Role of Rhetoric in Public Relations Theory and in Strategies of Corporate Discourse," *Journal of Communication Management*, May 2001, 6(2): 176–187.

5.   Winerip, op. cit., 72–74.

6.   Winerip, op. cit., 53.

CHAPTER 5

THE RISE OF ABNORMAL ACCIDENTS: A BRIEF HISTORY OF CRISES

> *... the Twentieth Century, from start to finish, has been character-*
> *ized by one act of genocide after another, committed by nationalist,*
> *secularist rulers. ...*
>
> *Between 1914 and 1945, seventy million people in Europe and*
> *the Soviet Union had died violent deaths.*
>
> *Source:* Karen Armstrong, *The Battle for God,* New York: Ballantine Books, 2000,
> p. 185.

Crises, catastrophes, and calamities are an unfortunate but inevitable fact of life. They have been with us since the beginning of time. It can be argued that they will be with us until the end of human history itself. In short, they are an integral part of the human condition. They *are* the human condition.

Nonetheless, there is something different about modern crises. They are as different as jets are from oxcarts.

By any measure, past crises and calamities took a horrendous toll on human lives. For instance, the Great Plague of 1665 and the Thirty Years' War from 1618 to 1648 claimed millions of lives. In addition, there is also no disputing the fact that the twentieth century invented one of the worst forms of evil, genocide, i.e., the deliberate destruction of whole groups of people merely because they were members of a particular ethnic group or race.

Nonetheless, past crises were primarily the result of natural disasters, such as the Great Plague or acts of war. Today's crises are caused by the effects of modern technology acting on scales previously unimaginable and by deliberate acts of evil carried out by means of the newest technologies. Whereas the first kind of crisis is generally unintentional, a by-product of the complexity of modern technology, the second is intentional and thereby evil.

Modern crises can be differentiated from past crises in terms of the scale on which they operate. For instance, a Chernobyl (the destruction of a Russian nuclear power plant in 1986) has the potential to affect the entire planet. As such, it is orders of magnitude greater in its destructive effects than the Thirty Years' War. For another, however horrific the Holocaust was—and there is no disputing this whatsoever—the

33

fear is that future forms of evil will be carried out against even larger populations, numbering in the hundreds of millions.

Nonetheless, the magnitude of crises cannot be compared merely by counting the number of people killed or injured. For instance, for a nation such as the United States that had not in almost two centuries been attacked directly on its mainland, the deaths of approximately 3,100 persons in the September 11, 2001, strikes against the New York World Trade Center Towers and the Pentagon, and the attempted strike against the White House, especially by means witnessed only before in disaster movies, cannot really be compared to other calamities. It is the events themselves that are horrific.

September 11 brought home the fact that the ability to wage war against whole populations has slipped into the hands of a relatively small number of people organized in new forms, terrorist cells, spread across the entire globe.[1] Whereas the Holocaust was organized primarily and directed by deranged government officials, today's crises are run by state-sponsored religious fundamentalists. This is not to say that today's fundamentalists do not aspire to take over entire countries and run them as religious states. They do. It is also not to deny that they wish to exterminate entire ethnic groups, for example, the Jewish people, and to wreak extreme havoc on Western nations and to destroy them.

Today's crises are the result of the coupling of modern technologies with ancient hatreds. We have no doubt that if previous generations had had access to modern technologies, they would have used them.

One thing is certain. Today's crises have the potential to rival natural disasters, and even acts of war, in their scope and magnitude.

For instance, Shrivastiva noted that between 1900 and 1987, 28 major industrial accidents occurred worldwide, where "major" is defined as 50 or more deaths.[2] The kicker in this statistic is that half of the 28 had occurred in the last 20 years, i.e., between 1967 and 1987. Not only has the size and scope of crises been increasing steadily, but the time between them has been decreasing precipitously.

Even if we cannot compare the magnitude of human tragedies in terms of numbers alone, we can trace their evolution. A timeline of recent crises indicates that all forms of crises have been increasing steadily.

A TIMELINE OF MAJOR CRISES

Figure 5.1 shows a timeline of major crises between 1979 and 2002. It reveals an ominous trend.

In 1984, Yale sociologist Charles Perrow published a highly influential book with the intriguing title *Normal Accidents.*[3] Through the study of several important industries such as airline, chemical, nuclear, and shipping, Perrow reached the conclusion that the potential for major crises, or catastrophes, was built into their basic operating structures. Because the systems and the technologies that were being managed were so complex, the potential for major accidents and catastrophes was extremely high, if not a virtual certainty. The central reason was that the management systems were not up to the task of managing the complex technologies. To put it mildly, the management systems were grossly inadequate. It was in this sense that catastrophic accidents were "normal."

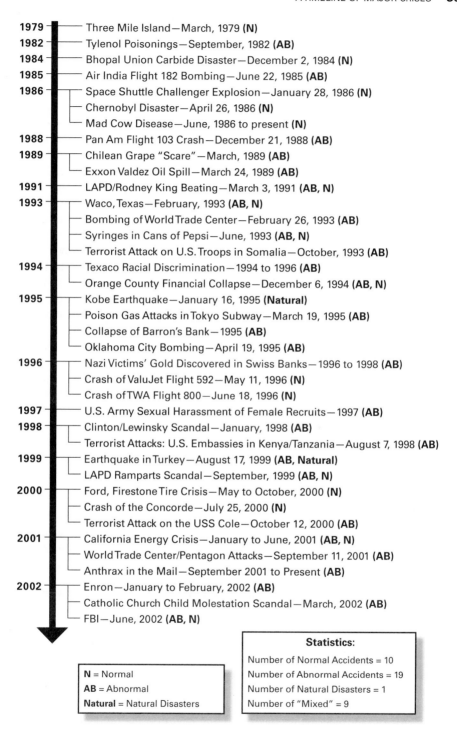

FIGURE 5-1 Timeline of Major Crises

While Perrow envisioned the possibility of terrorism directed, for instance, against nuclear power plants, terrorism was not yet the major force that it would become. For this reason, Perrow did not give equal consideration to what I call Abnormal Accidents or Evil Intentions. If Normal Accidents are the result of unintended evil, such as systems complexity, then Abnormal Accidents are the result of Evil Intentions, or deliberate acts of evil. In addition, there are of course also Natural Accidents, which are crises that result from natural disasters.

Although the classification is by no means exact, Figure 5.1 reveals that of the 39 major crises between 1979 and 2002, 10 can be classified as Normal, 19 as Abnormal, 1 as Natural, and 9 as a combination of Normal, Abnormal, and Natural forces acting simultaneously or in direct conjunction with one another. The figure reveals an ominous trend. While Normal and Abnormal Accidents are present throughout the entire time sequence, Normal Accidents are more prevalent in the beginning; Abnormal, more at the end.

The pattern also reveals a general increase in the scope, the size, and the impact of human-caused crises, both Normal and Abnormal. The pattern supports a contention made earlier in this chapter: For the first time in history, human-caused crises have the potential to exceed natural disasters in their scope, size, and impacts.

Human-caused crises have clearly entered into a new phase. It is one thing for catastrophes to occur as the result of improper human actions or inactions, coupled with the complexity of systems. It is quite another for them to occur as the result of evil intentions.

(The timeline of crises in Figure 5.1 must be taken with a strong word of caution. While I believe that the figure, and especially the implications that I have derived from it, are not artifacts, the determination of what is and what is not a "major crisis" is not without considerable argument. As we shall see, the definition of what is a crisis depends on the assumptions that one makes about a particular situation. For this reason, the definition of key terms is an important topic in itself.[4])

FAULTY ASSUMPTIONS

It would take us too far afield to examine every one of the crises listed in Figure 5.1. We need examine only a few in order to see the faulty assumptions upon which the systems that caused the crises were fashioned. As we stated earlier, the examination of basic assumptions is itself one of the most critical factors in Crisis Leadership. Indeed, it is one of the things that differentiates Crisis Management from Crisis Leadership. Every major crisis invalidates our most fundamental assumptions.

Tylenol

The Tylenol poisonings in suburbs of Chicago in 1982 are a landmark in the history of Crisis Management. It is generally acknowledged that the Tylenol poisonings were the start of the modern field of Crisis Management.

For years, food and pharmaceutical companies received threats in the mail to the effect that if certain financial demands were not met, then their products would be tampered with. The Tylenol case was the first time that a product was actually adulterated without a prior note to the company. As we shall examine later, there are exceedingly good reasons to believe that a psychopath or sociopath was involved. This examination will also help us understand the motives and mindset of terrorists.

The Tylenol poisonings invalidated a major assumption:

■ The future will be essentially like the past. Only those with a financial gain will make threats against food and pharmaceutical products. We are dealing with "rational" actors with whom we can bargain.

Three Mile Island

The Three Mile Island breakdown in 1979 was the worst nuclear accident in U.S. history. The major cause of the Pennsylvania accident was the improper design and layout of the operating panels in the control room of the power plant.

The control panels of the Three Mile Island nuclear reactor were not designed systematically by Human Factors engineers. Human Factors engineers, who are crucial in the design and the layout of complex equipment, ensure that dials and control panels are positioned so that they can be operated safely and properly by trained personnel.

At Three Mile Island, the control panels "just evolved" without any predictable or orderly design. On one panel, two gauges each with a red light were located side by side. On one gauge, a red light meant that the particular system was OK, but on the next dial, a red light meant that another system was operating in the danger zone. Even with extensive training, there is little chance that humans can operate such equipment safely, especially when they are stressed. In short, the layout of the control panels at Three Mile Island was a major contributing factor to the accident.

The major assumptions invalidated by Three Mile Island were:

■ It is sufficient for the design of critical control panels to "evolve at random"; and

■ Human operators can safely manage complex control panels without extensive training.

Bhopal

The catastrophe at Bhopal, India, is a prime illustration of faulty systems design coupled with poor management.[5] In 1984, a deadly gas, methyl isocyanate, was released into the atmosphere surrounding the plant due to operator error, faulty systems design, and poor plant management. As a result, 3,800 persons died and 2,720 suffered permanent disabilities.

The Bhopal plant was improperly designed from the beginning. Human errors were thus almost inevitable. In turn, human errors were exacerbated by the desire to cut operating costs. Indeed, the parent corporation, Union Carbide, deliberately terminated experienced personnel and hired inexperienced workers to oversee the plant. In addition, fewer numbers of personnel were rehired than had been fired.

A substantial part of the blame for the Bhopal catastrophe must be placed squarely on the Indian government. The Indian government allowed shantytowns to be built up to the edge of the plant without warning people that dangerous chemicals were being manufactured within the plant. In large part, this was because the government both highly desired the income the plant produced and did not want to scare off American corporations from operating in the Third World.

The effects of the Bhopal catastrophe were made even worse by the evasion of responsibility by both Union Carbide and the Indian government. Union Carbide staunchly refused to accept responsibility, saying that the most likely cause was employee sabotage. Even if this were the case, it only raises the question, "If sabotage was so important and highly likely, why then wasn't it considered in the basic design of the plant?"

The major operating assumption invalidated by Bhopal was:

■   Inexperienced personnel can safely operate poorly designed, complex systems.

The Challenger

The explosion of the space shuttle Challenger soon after liftoff in January 1986 is on the borderline between a complex systems accident, or Normal Accident, and an Abnormal Accident.[6]

Within the National Aeronautics and Space Administration (NASA), it was well known that below 35 degrees Fahrenheit, the infamous O-ring that was supposed to prevent fumes from getting to the rockets was improperly designed. As a result, it failed to do its basic job. Even worse, it seems that personnel within NASA colluded actively in preventing this critical information from getting from the bottom of the organization to those at the top, where the "correct decisions" would presumably be made. Thus, not only was the booster rocket imperfectly designed, but so was NASA's organizational structure.

Another major contributing cause of the accident was political pressure to fly the shuttle within a narrow time slot. This contributed to the syndrome of "poor overall managerial decision making." Throughout the Challenger episode, we can see a theme that reverberates throughout this book: the interplay between complex systems and equally complex, if not faulty, organizations.

A major assumption invalidated by the Challenger disaster was:

■   Complex technologies can be safely operated independently of the particular organizations in which they are embedded.

Orange County

Orange County, California, illustrates another major type. In particular, it illustrates what we call "weird coupling."

"Weird coupling" is a central feature of Normal Accidents. However, the Orange County fiasco introduces a novel wrinkle.

Orange County was the first in U.S. history to default on its payments. This was due to the failure of extremely risky investments made by Orange County's treasurer, Robert Citron.

Let us trace the chain of events. Basically, Citron was responding, all too well, to the "underlying needs of the public." The citizens of Orange County wanted high levels of county service while at the same time paying low taxes. Citron more than delivered on this desire. He invested county money in extremely high-risk bonds. As long as the bonds were producing income, things ran smoothly. But when they defaulted, so did Citron and Orange County.

Here is where "weird coupling" entered into the equation. Many of the investments that Citron made were in Japanese securities. When the Kobe earthquake occurred, a major Natural Disaster, money from these investments was "called in" to provide relief for the victims. This resulted in the "financial bottom falling out of Orange County."

A major assumption invalidated by the Orange County fiasco was:

■   Normal and abnormal accidents are independent; the technology of complex systems is independent of the social milieu in which they reside.

As we shall see when we examine additional crises later in this book, other key assumptions were invalidated by other crises.

CONCLUDING REMARKS

We have entered irreversibly a world of complex systems. If this weren't bad enough, we have entered a world of complex systems that are coupled with unthinkable and unspeakable acts. The end result is a double whammy: We have Abnormal Forces acting in conjunction with Normal Accidents.

To be perfectly clear, I have not argued that barbarism and savagery are anything new. If anything, it is only the means of delivery and the scale on which they can be delivered that are new. This is what makes preparing for the unthinkable more urgent than ever before.

In times of great crisis, a natural tendency is to look for causes of evil that are external to us. This strategy tends to locate the causes as being *solely* external to us. The danger is that it inevitably downplays the role of internal factors.

For instance, consider the 2002 Winter Olympics in Salt Lake City, Utah. These Olympics are a prime illustration of the need for *equal* preparation for both internal and external crises. While hundreds of millions of dollars were spent on preparation for external terrorist threats, it was the failure to deal with internal factors that marred the image of the Games. It is difficult for organizations to be prepared equally for both internal and external crises.

To be as clear as possible, I am *not* denying that external factors were primarily responsible for 9/11. I am also *not* denying that the terrorists responsible for these factors should be brought to justice. They should!

My point is that if we focus solely on external factors, then we will fail to treat the full sources that are responsible for the crises we face. The design and the operation of our organizations and institutions, both public and private, are a major source of the problem. Unless we fundamentally redesign our major organizations and institutions, we will only perpetuate our vulnerabilities.

EXERCISES

1. Describe the critical differences between Normal, Natural, and Abnormal crises or disasters.

2. Illustrate how Normal, Natural, and Abnormal disasters can interact or overlap. Illustrate how a Natural Disaster can lead to both Normal and Abnormal disasters.

3. Are there critical differences in how an organization needs to prepare for Normal, Natural, and Abnormal accidents? Why?

NOTES

1. Talbott, Strobe, and Chanda, Nyan (eds.), *The Age of Terror,* New York: Basic Books, 2001.
2. See Shrivastiva, Paul, *Bhopal: Anatomy of a Disaster,* New York: Ballinger, 1987.
3. Perrow, Charles, *Normal Accidents: Living with High Risk Technologies,* New York: Basic Books, 1984.
4. See Mitroff, Ian I., and Linstone, Harold A., *The Unbounded Mind,* New York: Oxford University Press, 1993.
5. Shrivastava, op. cit.
6. Perrow, Charles, "The President's Commission and the Normal Accident," in D. Sills, C. Wolf, and V. Shelanski (eds.), *The Accident at Three Mile Island: The Human Dimensions*, Boulder, CO: Westview Press, 1981, 173–184.; Starbuck, W.H., and Milliken, F.J., "Challenger: Finetuning the Odds Until Something Breaks," *Journal of Management Studies,* 1988, 25: 319–340; Vaughan, D., "Autonomy, Interdependence and Social Control: NASA and the Space Shuttle Challenger," *Administrative Science Quarterly,* 1990, 35: 225–257.

CHAPTER 6

THE DIFFERENT LANGUAGES OF MANAGERS AND EXECUTIVES: THE PERSONALITIES OF INDIVIDUALS

> *... the big picture is precisely what [William Clay Ford, Jr., Chairman of Ford Motor Company] missed. He seemed to have misjudged the magnitude and gravity of the [Firestone/Ford tire] crisis. It wasn't until well into August that it became apparent to him that his company's reputation was at stake. Firestone began claiming that the design of the Explorer—its thin roof and tendency to roll over—was a contributing factor to highway deaths. This warring between the companies resulted in two Congressional investigations and a dangerous public-relations predicament for Ford.*
>
> Source: Martha Sherrill, "The Buddha of Detroit," *New York Times Magazine,* November 26, 2000, p.115.

With this chapter, we begin our detailed examination of the skills that are essential to Crisis Leadership. We begin with the fundamental issue of *individual* personality differences. As we shall see in the next chapter, *organizations* also exhibit different personalities.

As complex as individuals and organizations are, the differences between them can be captured in a relatively small number of dimensions. The personality differences between individuals and organizations significantly affect how they plan for, respond to, and even think about crises.

THE MYERS-BRIGGS PERSONALITY TEST

Over the years, the author and his colleagues have used the Myers-Briggs Personality Test to characterize and to study individuals and organizations.[1] The Myers-Briggs Personality Test is based on the pioneering discoveries and work of the great Swiss psychoanalyst Çarl Jung.[2] For in-depth understanding of Jung and Myers-Briggs, the reader is referred to the references at the end of this chapter.[3] To further the reader's understanding, it is strongly recommended that he or she take the Myers-Briggs before reading this chapter.

The Myers-Briggs is certainly not the only personality test that can be used to capture individual and organizational differences. Furthermore, it is certainly not the only reliable and valid descriptor of human behavior. It is, however, one of the easiest to explain to a diverse set of people and to use in describing individual and organizational personality differences.

To see how personality differences bear directly on the world of work, consider one manager's reflections:

> One of the hardest things that I had to learn as a manager was that people didn't all speak the same language. It was not only very difficult to make sense of these different languages, but it was even harder to learn to respect all of them as equally valid ways of responding to and describing the world. In fact, I found that the second difficulty was a real barrier to my learning to understand the different languages in the first place. If you don't respect the way a person looks at the world, how can you really understand the language they speak?
>
> By "language," I don't mean English, French, or Japanese. I mean the ways that different people view the world. The "languages" people speak are a direct reflection of how they view reality. They are their reality!
>
> For instance, some people naturally speak the language of "hard facts." Others speak the language of "future possibilities and hypothetical what/ifs." What is "real" to one person is not to another.
>
> For some people, facts are knowledge and truth. For others, possibilities are. For the latter, they prefer to base their business plans and sales projections on what their gut tells them.
>
> I had to learn that there was a place for both types in my organization even if they could not always work closely together. You need the types of people who see possibilities when you're in the brainstorming part of a project. They open up new, creative, and exciting ideas. They don't censor themselves merely because something isn't true at the present time. However, when you get to the feasibility part, i.e., what actually can be done and how much it will cost, then you have to involve people who are good with facts.
>
> Both of them have their place, but not necessarily in the same type of job. As a manager, one of the most critical things you have to know is which kind of person is right for which kind of job, and for which kind of organization.
>
> I also had to learn that it took a lot of explaining and a lot of off-site retreats for different types of people to appreciate one another and to work together. In fact, some people never could get beyond their differences. For this reason, unless there was a job in which they could work entirely by themselves, I had to let them go. They were just too rigid in their ways. Their way of looking at things was *the only* way. That is not

acceptable in any organization that is composed of a variety of different people with whom one *has* to get along.

A FAILURE TO COMMUNICATE

Four citizens are having an important argument about a tragedy that has affected their community: the growing number of deaths of children at unprotected railroad and streetcar crossings.

Carol, the first person to speak, has been arguing that the way to prevent the problem is to install better security and protective devices on both the trains and at the crossings. Her focus is exclusively on security and protective devices. She also focuses entirely on current technology. Furthermore, since Carol is extremely practical and not future-oriented, her emphasis is on the here-and-now, i.e., things that can be put into practice almost immediately.

Susan, the next person to jump into the debate, focuses on the latest technology. Susan is so future-oriented that without losing a beat she leaps naturally to the reinvention of "trains" and "crossings." In other words, Susan instinctively thinks "outside the box." She looks to new technology to prevent the problem in the first place.

Brent, the next person to speak, focuses instinctively on the problem as one of setting up appropriate "community watch groups" who will go daily to the most dangerous intersections and help children cross safely. Brent instinctively visualizes all of the "new human linkages" that can be forged between independent community groups to create a new "community awareness."

Finally, Tom, the last person to speak, focuses on one child and one family alone that has experienced a tragedy at a particular crossing. Tom wants to conduct day and night vigils in order to dramatize the tragedy. He is not concerned with families or communities in the abstract or large, but rather, with the loss of *one* child and its impact on *one* family. Tom wants to take a picture of a child and his or her family and put it at the site where the child was killed in order to focus public attention and to mourn the loss of a single human being.

As is typical of so many arguments, each person fails to convince the others to see his or her point of view. It is as if each of them is speaking a totally different language. The result is that no one convinces the others, and each leaves with a deep sense of frustration.

The Varieties of English

For years, I have been working with people from all walks of life to help them understand the different psychological languages they speak and how to bridge them. Since English is for the most part their native tongue, they start out assuming, erroneously, that they are all speaking the same language. They assume, again erroneously, that the same English words have a common meaning.

The situation is far worse than if they were speaking different foreign languages. In that case, they wouldn't hesitate to involve a translator to resolve the likely difficulties in communication. But since they are all speaking English, it doesn't occur to them that they need a translator even more. If a person doesn't attach the same meanings to a word that someone else does, the natural tendency is for each person to regard the other as "just plain wrong." At best, there is confusion. If both of them are assigned to work on a common task, it is extremely difficult for them to function as a cohesive team. They constant fight over the "correct meaning" of words.

There is no doubt that the decoding of language is fundamental to understanding how individuals and organizations experience and think about reality. Furthermore, the notion that each of us is unique is just as fundamental. Thus, understanding the different languages that people speak is absolutely essential if we are to respect and tolerate the uniqueness of every individual.

FOUR KINDS OF UNIQUENESS

An old philosophical joke goes as follows: "There are two kinds of people: those who think that there are two kinds of people and those who don't!" Not only is it a common tendency to put people into "boxes," but as soon as we have, it is just as common to ridicule our classification schemes. There is something deep within us all that wants and needs classification, and at the same time despises it.

For our purposes in this book, we are going to describe four kinds of people and hence four distinct kinds of uniqueness. Paradoxically, "uniqueness" follows a "general pattern."

Although there are obviously more than four kinds of people, we are going to discuss four broad and distinct styles of relating to the world. If everything were so distinct that it couldn't even be described, then communication would be impossible. The notion of language already presupposes shared, general classification schemes. If there were no such schemes, then every one of us would have to invent the word "horse," for example, every time we needed it.

Four Psychological Languages[4]

The first critical difference between those who speak a different "psychological language" is between those who instinctively frame every problem or issue in terms of "things" versus those who frame every problem or issue in terms of "people." For brevity, I will call the language of those who speak in terms of "things" or objects Thing. (Jung labels this aspect of personality Thinking. Since Jung and the Myers-Briggs Personality Test are used widely, I shall use both labels Thing and Thinking to refer to the same personality characteristic.)

Thing uses science and technology to address every problem and issue. In contrast, the opposite language uses emotions and feelings to address every problem and issue. I shall call this opposite language People. (Jung and Myers-Briggs refer to this personality characteristic as Feeling. Feeling is not to be confused with emotion. All of the various personality types can be extremely emotional in describing and defending their particular view of the world. Thus, Feeling is a special way of relating to the world. It is not necessarily emotional.)

Those who speak Thing typically use impersonal numbers and statistics to represent the "true, underlying nature" of any problem or situation. For instance, in any crisis, there are undeniable economic aspects and consequences. That is, whatever a company does in the heat of a crisis threatens to affect its bottom line significantly. There is no way to ignore the economics of any business situation, crisis or otherwise.

While economic considerations are certainly an important aspect of every problem and situation, people who speak Thing regard the economic, technical, and scientific aspects of problems and situations as their only essential and true characteristics. They not only perceive the economic, technical, and scientific aspects of problems first and foremost, but they regard those aspects as the only legitimate and true aspects. People who speak Thing justify it as the only language that provides a "true and objective" description of reality. It doesn't matter that their position is tautological or circular, for this misses the main point.

What is at stake is not an abstract philosophical discussion, or metaphysical discourse, with regard to the "real, underlying" nature of things.[5] Instead, a psychological representation of the world is unconsciously being assumed and defended. The language of Thing is not a description of the "world" as it "is," but rather as it appears to those who speak Thing. Thing satisfies deep psychological needs for orderliness, predictability, and certainty.

In contrast, people who speak People talk primarily about, and are oriented to, human concerns and feelings. Such people "feel instinctively" that to always use the impersonal language of economics serves in the long run only to alienate a business from its customers.

It is of the utmost importance to realize that neither of these languages, Thing or People, is "more real," "more fundamental," or "more important" than the other. Both are psychological orientations to the world. They describe the persons using them more than they do reality.

Both languages are needed in describing the "true nature" and the "full complexity" of every situation. As the quotation from the manager at the front of this chapter illustrates, outstanding managers and executives understand this implicitly. They understand how people become the prisoners of the languages in which they are ensconced. Without trying to convert people from one language to another, such managers and executives attempt to bridge the different languages that people speak. Gently and firmly, they attempt to get each person to see the "world" of the other. In doing this, they do not use violent or abrasive means. Instead, over time, they provide ways so that the languages of Thing and People can be integrated.

This does not mean that a staunch Thing or People person ultimately will not have to be terminated. This is especially the case if their language is so ingrained that it completely shuts a person off from respecting the language of others. Unless a staunch speaker of a particular language can work completely isolated, then all of us invariably have to confront the fact that people do not use words in the same way. It is even harder to accept the notion that both languages are describing an aspect of reality and not the whole of it.

The point of this discussion is not to put people into narrow and rigid categories or boxes. Its purpose is to make the point that people have a natural tendency to gravitate toward the use of one language. This does not mean that there are no persons who can understand and speak both languages. If there were none, there would be no such thing as "organization bridge builders." Organization bridge builders serve the extremely important function of translating between the languages that people use.

At the current point in world history, the number of persons who can bridge both languages are still relatively rare. This does not mean that the prospect for their increase is dim. There are in fact good reasons to believe just the opposite. The prospects for the increase in the numbers of people who can bridge both languages are actually quite good.[6]

Details/Parts versus the Big Picture

In addition to speaking Thing or People, individuals tend to speak two additional languages as well: Detail/Parts versus the Big Picture. People who speak the language of Details generally take a complex situation and break it down into components or parts. They then focus on the parts as if the whole were nothing more than its parts, not even its sum. All of "reality" is located in the parts. (Jung refers to Detail/Parts as Sensing or Sensations. In contrast, Jung calls the Big Picture Intuition.)

To a certain extent, this makes sense. We are surrounded by complex problems that transcend national boundaries. These problems are so enormously complex that there is little wonder that people want to take refuge in tiny bits that they can seemingly manage. In addition, people tend to think that the smaller the problem and the more confined its boundaries, the more likely it is that precise scientific and objective data can be gathered on it. This is the thinking of people who are Detail or Part oriented.

At the other end of the spectrum are the Big Picture people. Their attitude is completely reversed. Unless one sees how all the component parts fit together into a larger whole or pattern, then by themselves the parts are completely meaningless.

Outstanding managers and executives do not take sides in this important debate. They know that both languages are necessary. Every problem and situation can be reduced to and looked at from the standpoint of its separate parts. How one initially divides something into up its "parts," however, depends on the particular analyst and his or her discipline or corporate function. We would not expect a financial division of the world to look the same as a marketing or public affairs division. What one sees as the components or parts depends on who is doing the dissection. Every division of a whole into its parts depends on how we first look at the whole, and vice versa. There is no way of getting out of this conundrum.

We can combine these four kinds of language, or dimensions as to how people view reality, to arrive at four major psychological languages as shown in Figure 6.1. That is, managers and executives speak at least the following four: (1) Detail-Thing or Sensing-Thinking; (2) Big Picture–Thing or Intuiting-Thinking; (3) Big Picture–People or Intuiting-Feeling; and (4) Detail-People or Sensing-Feeling. Since the symbol I is used for Introvert in the Jung/Myers-Briggs system (E is used for Extrovert), the symbol N is used for Intuition. In short, the four languages are: (1) ST, (2) NT, (3) NF, and (4) SF.

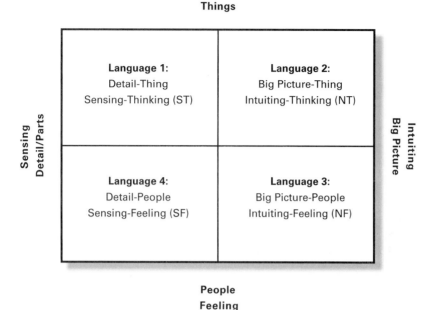

FIGURE 6-1   The Four Languages of Managers and Executives

Psychological Jobs

Figure 6.2 shows some of the corporate functions, or jobs, that are typically associated with each of each of the four basic languages. Each of the functions or jobs is also a prime example of the kind of psychological language that is spoken by representatives of each of the four cells or quadrants in Figure 6.2.

Auditors and Financial Analysts typically speak the psychological language of impersonal Details, Facts, and Things. No matter the particular issue or situation, they prefer to gather detailed facts, and then apply impersonal, scientifically validated ways of analyzing the facts to reach a general conclusion. The ideal is a general formula that can be applied to all situations no matter what their specifics.

Unless detailed Facts can be gathered and unless a general formula can be applied, Detail-Thing people, or STs, regard the situation as hopelessly vague and subjective. As a result, it is not worthy of serious consideration. According to this way of thinking, how can one conduct a meaningful analysis of a situation if it cannot be reduced to Facts and if it cannot be analyzed according to a General Impersonal Formula that applies to all people in similar situations? According to this way of thinking, not only can everything in the universe be reduced to its Detailed Parts and Things, but it must be if one is to stand any chance of having a "scientific" discussion about it. In this sense, the language of science and technology is the only valid way of looking at things.

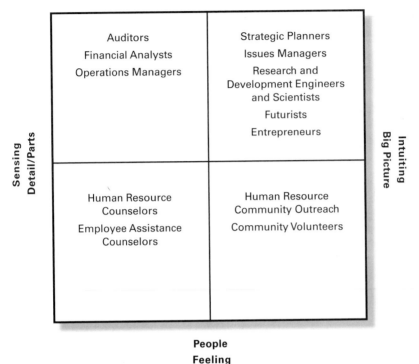

FIGURE 6-2 Major Corporate Functions and Occupations

Strategic planners, research engineers, and scientists typically speak the language of Big Picture-Thing, or NT. Since by definition the future has not yet occurred, strategic planners and researchers have to speak in terms of hypotheticals, what-ifs, and multiple scenarios. They have to consider multiple alternatives or futures. It just comes with the territory. They cannot be bound to a single set of facts or a single way of looking at any problem or situation.

For each separate set of facts, or different way of looking at a situation, they prefer to analyze each of them in terms of impersonal multiple formulas. According to this way of looking at the world, why indeed shouldn't each separate scenario have its own special formula? Thus, while strategic planners and researchers still speak the language of Thing, it is best referred to as Multiple Thing.

Human Resource planners, especially those with a focus on Community Outreach, also speak the language of hypotheticals, what-ifs, and future scenarios and possibilities. However, in this case, the scenarios are not impersonal. They are loaded with concepts and words that pertain to people. They typically use such terms as "concern," "community orientation," " humanity," and "trust."

The major difference between the bottom two quadrants is as follows: Human Resource people with a Community Outreach focus, i.e., NFs, consider the Whole System. In this case, they focus on the largest human groups possible—in the extreme, humankind or humanity. On the other hand, Human Resource people with a focus on Details or Parts, or SFs, concentrate on specific individuals. In this case, Details are no longer viewed as Impersonal Facts, but instead as specific, living, breathing individuals. Such people typically approach Human Resource issues from an individual Counseling perspective.

The metaphor that best describes people in the lower left-hand quadrant is Family. The metaphor that best describes people in the lower right-hand quadrant is either Community or Humanity. The metaphor that best describes people in the upper right-hand quadrant is Systems Thinkers. The metaphor that best describes people in the upper left-hand quadrant is Optimizers, or believers in the Single, One Best Way, or One Best Answer.

The Structure of Needs

Figures 6.1 and 6.2 are indispensable in explaining the complex structure of human needs, and, why they are organized in terms of opposites. That is, even though most people gravitate toward one particular quadrant of Figures 6.1 and 6.2, they have needs that fall into the quadrants opposite from them as well.

If one looks at the upper left-hand quadrant of Figures 6.1 and 6.2, the emphasis of people who typify this way of speaking are concerned with the articulation of clear, consistent rules and structures that apply universally. In short, their life is governed by the search for *the* Formula, a "one size fits all" approach to life. What they are responding to is the human need for setting limits, specifying clear boundaries, outlining clear rules and procedures, building systematic structures, and setting clear agendas. They run into trouble when they take their notion of structure as the only kind of possible structure. In their thinking, everything must be organized hierarchically. At best, people in the upper left-hand quadrant respond to the persistent need for clarity, consistency, and structure.

The persons in the upper right-hand quadrant are responding to the human need for comprehensiveness, the need to look at the Bigger Picture, to see the Whole System. It is not enough to understand anything if one merely looks at it independently of its connections to everything else. The people in the upper right-hand quadrant see not only the Big Picture, but also the connections. Indeed, for them the connections are everything.

The people in the lower right-hand quadrant see not only the Big Picture, but also people in their "largest dimension." As a result, they are the antithesis of the people in the upper left-hand quadrant.

The people who are represented by the two diagonals in Figures 6.1 and 6.2 are the antitheses of one another. Because they differ on each of the separate psychological dimensions, they share no common "dictionary" or "language." No wonder they often experience serious difficulties in getting along.

The people in the bottom left-hand quadrant focus on Details in the form of specific individuals. As such, they are the antithesis of the people in the upper right-hand quadrant. Once again, they share no common "dictionary" or "language."

Even though most people tend to fall in one or two cells or quadrants at best, they have underlying needs expressed by the opposite cells or quadrants. In other words, all of us do ourselves and others a great disservice when we neglect the opposite and often "unconscious" needs in the other cells.

AN EXAMPLE

One of the best ways—often, the only way—to understand these four languages is to go through the exercise of treating a complex problem from the vantage point of each language. For this reason, I insist that people bring with them concrete problems to whatever seminar I am conducting. The problem can be from their organizations, their families, or from the general news of the day. All that matters is that they be willing to discuss it.

For instance, let us go back to the problem with which we started this chapter, the death of children at unprotected railroad and streetcar crossings. Detail-Thing people, or STs, reduce this problem to microtechnology such as installing better security and protective devices on the trains and at the crossings themselves. As we noted, their focus is exclusively on security and protective devices. Their focus is also on current technology.

In contrast, Big Picture-Thing people, or NTs, focus on new technologies. For this reason, they even try to reinvent the notion of "trains" and "crossings" so that they can bring fresh perspectives to the problem. They are the premier example of thinking outside of the dots or boxes.

Big Picture-People people, or NFs, focus on the problem as one of setting up community watch groups who will help children across the tracks safely. They form human and political linkages between independent community groups to forge a new community awareness.

Finally, Detail-People people, or SFs, focus on one child and one family that has experienced a tragedy at a particular crossing. They want to conduct day and night vigils to dramatize the tragedy. They are not concerned with families or communities in the abstract, but instead with the loss of one child and the accident's impact on one family.

By now, it should be obvious that all four of these perspectives are needed in forming any true and lasting solution to the problem. Indeed, any single solution is dependent upon all of the others in order for it to work. For instance, no matter how good technology may be, it always depends on people to run it. For another, the design of a particular technology always depends on the people who have the problem and will use the technology.

What is especially interesting is that each of these four perspectives not only "solves" the problem in an entirely different way, but also "formulates" it differently in the first place. *The solution of a problem is not independent of how we formulate it.* This is precisely one of the things that occurs by being able to look at four different views of a problem. The ability to look at a problem from multiple perspectives is absolutely essential if one wants to avoid falling into the trap of "solving the wrong problem precisely."[7]

THE ESSENTIAL ROLE OF MANAGERS AND EXECUTIVES

Outstanding managers and executives are not trapped into using any of the four languages in Figures 6.1 and 6.2. As a result, they are not the prisoners of any one of these languages. Indeed, they see the absolute necessity of being fluent in every one of them simultaneously. In other words, they realize that all of us have needs that fall into every one of the quadrants in Figures 6.1 and 6.2. They also respect the tension between opposing needs.

One of the fundamental conflicts with which humans must constantly struggle is the perpetual tension between the need for structure and stability on the one hand and for constant change and novelty on the other. This tension is represented by the two diagonals in Figures 6.1 and 6.2. The upper left-hand quadrant with its extreme emphasis on hierarchy, structure, and stability is the opposite of the lower right-hand quadrant with its emphasis on the flexibility, openness, and people.

Outstanding managers and executives realize that it is *never* an either/or but *always* a both/and. They constantly try to bring together both aspects in any problem or situation. They endlessly try to translate and to communicate between each of the psychological languages. They realize that each language addresses a vital aspect of reality. They also realize that "human reality" is not contained solely within any one of the individual quadrants, but is a property of the framework as a whole.

Figures 6.1 and 6.2 provide not only a way to understand the languages that divide people, but also a way to bridge those languages. Nonetheless, "bridging" is extremely difficult. People have to come to understand their own language as well as the validity of another way of looking at the world. (We discuss "bridging" later in this chapter; in particular, see Figure 6.3.) As difficult as this may be, bridging is one of the supreme tasks of management. Unless one hires people from just one quadrant, which can be disastrous to an organization because it will not pick up information that any whole organism needs to function, it has to learn how to communicate with people with opposite views.

OTHER CONSIDERATIONS

A number of current books contain good advice, if not downright common sense, with regard to how to manage effectively.[8] For instance, in order to perform their jobs correctly, people need the right tools, the right workspaces, clear recognition and rewards, the setting of appropriate goals and objectives, appropriate down or rest time, the opportunity to socialize on and off the job, a shared vision of their organization, the direction in which their work unit and organization is going, and an appropriate organizational structure in which to work. For the most part, none of these considerations has been related to Figures 6.1 and 6.2. It is assumed that the tools appropriate for one psychological language are appropriate for another. The same thing is true for all the other concepts such as work space, recognition/rewards, and so forth.

The "tools" appropriate for one kind of job or person are not necessarily appropriate for another, and certainly not for all organizations.[9] For instance, there is no doubt that Auditors need appropriate audit tools. Computer spreadsheets and software are critical in performing the job of an Auditor. However, people in the other quadrants need other kinds of "tools." For instance, people in the lower right-hand quadrant need a way of "visualizing" the existence of and the relationships between different stakeholders that compose a community. They need to know which government and community agencies can be turned to when an employee has a critical medical or psychological condition. This knowledge is a different kind of tool.

As important as it is to note that people need the appropriate tools in order to perform their jobs, it is equally important to note that different jobs demand different kinds of tools. Without that recognition, the implication is that there is only one set of tools, i.e., one size fits all. This is contrary to the advice in those books that everyone is different and must be treated as a unique individual.[10]

THE PROBLEM WITH ORGANIZATIONAL PROGRAMS

Few organizational programs are initiated with all four languages explicitly in mind. For instance, consider Total Quality Management, or TQM. To my knowledge, Ralph Kilmann is one of the few persons to have considered an integrated TQM from the standpoint of all four of the languages in Figures 6.1 and 6.2.[11]

For the most part, TQM is presented either as a body of statistical and manufacturing techniques, or as a set of organizational and cultural practices. This is downright perverse, since some of TQM's leading proponents have proposed systems that, at least in a minimal sense, attempt to bridge the four. Without an explicit awareness of Figures 6.1 and 6.2, it is at best happenstance that an integration will be effected.

THE MAIN LESSON

The main lesson of this chapter is that all four concerns must be addressed explicitly and systematically for any important management initiative to succeed. This fact alone almost explains the failure of most fads. Fads primarily come out of only one of the four languages in Figures 6.1 and 6.2.

SPEAKING THE LANGUAGE OF MANAGEMENT

Figure 6.3 is a compact summary of how to "speak" the language of each of the four psychological "realities" we have been discussing. By implication, Figure 6.3 also shows how to bridge these languages. That is, in order for someone in the upper left-hand quadrant to speak to somebody in the upper right-hand, then the language of Detail-Thing, or ST, must be willing to "loosen" or to "broaden" its hold on specifics and details. It must be not only encouraged but also rewarded to see that nothing dire will happen if one does not approach a problem in excruciating detail.

Stern
Things/Thinking

Give Lots of Facts, Numbers, Details, and Specifics Give Step-By-Step Procedures for Solving the Problem Give Detailed Time Schedules When the Solution is Expected Indicate Clearly What the Rewards Are for Solving Specific Problems	Engage the Creative Imagination of People in Formulating the Problem in Diverse and Multiple Ways Reward Ideas and Possibilities. Reward People for New and Creative Ways of Formulating the Problem Reward People for "Break Out" Strategies
Encourage People to Trust their Feelings Encourage People to Develop Specific Relationships Encourage Them to Share Their Personal Concerns About Their Family Problems Encourage Them to Share and to Tell Personal "Stories" that Illuminate a Situation Encourage Them to State Personal Considerations that will Improve the Work Environment	Reward and Encourage People for Reaching Out to the Wider Community, if not to Worldwide Agencies Reward and Encourage the Building of Community Relationships and Partnerships Encourage Volunteerism Encourage and Reward Looking at the Organization as a Total "Living" System

Left axis: **Managers** — Detail/Parts Sensing

Right axis: **Leaders** — Big Picture Intuiting

People/Feeling
Nurturer

FIGURE 6-3   The Four Languages of Managers and Executives

Conversely, those in the upper right-hand quadrant must be encouraged to provide more details and specifics with regard to a particular problem if they are to engage the psychological cooperation of people in the upper left-hand quadrant.

This is precisely what outstanding managers and executives strive to accomplish. This is why they are so invaluable.

CONCLUDING REMARKS

The framework introduced in this chapter is extremely powerful. It captures a great deal of what goes on in organizations. For instance, Figure 6.3 shows four additional dimensions that are associated with different styles of managing. Immediately above the word "Thing" is the label "Stern." By the same token, immediately to the side of each of the labels we have been discussing are additional ones in bold that pertain to management.

Consider the horizontal dimension, Managers versus Leaders. The eminent management consultant Peter Drucker has described the differences between the two extremely well. As Drucker has put it, "Managers do 'things right' whereas Leaders determine what are the 'right things' to do in the first place." The point is not only that there are distinct styles of running organizations, but also that Managers naturally attend to details whereas Leaders see the Big Picture.

By the same token, there is a difference between those who naturally adopt a Stern, or Parental, attitude toward managing versus those who develop a Nurturing approach. Those who promote a Stern approach focus on rules, whereas those who adopt a Nurturing approach attend to emotions and feelings.

All organizations need a mixture of all four approaches if they are to survive and prosper.[12]

EXERCISES

1. Go back to Chapter Four and examine the general pattern in which all crises, especially those that are mismanaged, follow. Match each of the various aspects of the general pattern in Chapter Four to Figures 6.1 and 6.2. What is the relationship between the elements of the general pattern to the four languages that were presented in this chapter? Do the elements of the general pattern tend to fall in certain quadrants more than others? Why?
2. In which quadrant of Figure 6.1 and 6.2 would you place Risk Management? Why?
3. Go through each of the quadrants or "languages" that were presented in this chapter and specify how each would treat crises. That is, what aspect of Crisis Leadership is each language addressing? From this examination, what can you conclude about the scope of Crisis Leadership? Does this give you an understanding as to why Crisis Leadership is so difficult to practice? Why?
4. What kind of crises do you think that each quadrant from Figures 6.1 and 6.2 is most likely to treat?

NOTES

1.   See Mitroff, Ian I., *Stakeholders of the Organizational Mind: Toward a New View of Policy Making,* San Francisco: Jossey-Bass, 1983.

2.   See Jung, C.G., *The Collected Works of Carl Jung*, Volume 6: Psychological Types, edited and translated by Gerhard Adler and R.F.C. Hull, Princeton, NJ: Princeton University Press, 1971; see also Myers, Isabel Briggs, *Gifts Differing*, Palo Alto, CA: Consulting Psychologists Press, 1980.

3.   See Mitroff, op. cit.

4.   This section uses the Jungian, or Myers-Briggs, Personality "Types" or system; see Isabel Briggs Myers, op. cit.

5.   For a discussion of metaphysics in everyday life, see Mitroff, Ian I., and Linstone, Harold A., *The Unbounded Mind*, New York: Oxford University Press, 1992.

6.   Ken Wilber, *A Brief Theory of Everything*, Boston: Shambhala, 1996.

7.   See Mitroff and Linstone, op. cit.

8.   Buckingham, Marcus, and Coffman, Curt, *First, Break All the Rules: What the World's Greatest Managers Do Differently*, New York: Simon & Schuster, 1999; Spreitzer, Gretchen, and Quinn, Robert, *A Company of Leaders: Five Disciplines for Unleashing the Power of Your Workforce*, San Francisco: Jossey-Bass, 2001.

9.   Chatman, J.A., "Matching People and Organizations: Selection and Socialization in Public Accounting Firms," *Administrative Science Quarterly*, 1991, 36: 459–484.

10.   Ibid.

11.   Kilmann, Ralph, *Quantum Organizations: A New Paradigm for Achieving Organizational Success and Personal Meaning*, Palo Alto, CA: Consulting Psychologists Press/Davies-Black Publishing, 2001.

12.   Schein, E.H., *Organizational Culture and Leadership*, San Francisco: Jossey-Bass, 1985.

CHAPTER 7

THE PERSONALITIES
OF ORGANIZATIONS

> *The broad ground rules that gave each intelligence bureaucracy its own role and swath of territory don't make much sense in the new war. The C.I.A. has largely stayed out of domestic intelligence gathering, in part because of limits set by Congress in the '70's to protect citizens from the agency's excesses, such as dosing unwitting subjects with L.S.D. During the Cold War and afterward, the Pentagon, F.B.I., and C.I.A. split the responsibility for tracking foreign threats, but each agency kept the others in the dark about what it was doing. That division of labor failed completely in spotting clues to Sept. 11, so it's good news that in the race to stop the next attack, the lines between fiefs have finally started to blur.*
>
> Source: Massimo Calabresi and Romesh Ratnesar, "Can We Stop the Next Attack?" *TIME,* March 11, 2002, p. 30.

The results of the previous chapter apply not only to individuals but to organizations as well. Organizations have "personalities" in the same ways that individuals do.[1] To see this, consider the following exercise that the author and his colleagues have used over the years to make the concepts behind Figures 6.1 and 6.2 readily apparent.

WHAT TINKER TOYS REVEAL ABOUT ORGANIZATIONS

Suppose for the sake of argument that we have a group of 40 people. Suppose further that the group is equally divided among the four major Jungian or Myers-Briggs types. That is, ten are STs; ten are NTs; ten are NFs; and ten are SFs. We put all of the STs in one group; all of the NTs in another, etc. We give each group a set of Tinker Toys and ask them to build something that represents their "ideal organization." Finally, we ask them to give a name to their Tinker Toy construction and to list as many characteristics of their ideal organization as possible.

The advantages of this exercise are as follows:

- Putting all of the people with the same personality type in the same group generally magnifies the group's way of looking at the world; i.e., it intensifies what they share;
- It magnifies the differences between the groups;

- Asking each group to build something allows us to *see* personality. By definition, "personality" is "internal" to people; for this reason, it is difficult to put one's finger on it;

- Since each group starts with a similar set of Tinker Toys and since there are generally no "experts" in Tinker Toys, each group is free to project its internal personality onto its construction; and

- Asking each group to give its construction a name and to list its properties draws out further personality traits and hence the differences between groups.

The results of the exercise are shown in Figure 7.1. The ideal organization of STs is the classic or traditional bureaucracy.[2] It reflects the ST's underlying desire for certainty, exactness, order, and precision. It also reflects an impersonal orientation to the world.

The ideal organization of STs is a bureaucracy, since in this kind of organization everyone "knows exactly what is expected of them at all times." In the ideal bureaucracy, there are no uncertainties. Everyone's job is completely defined. In addition, everyone knows exactly to whom they report and on what scales or "metrics" they will be evaluated. Consistent with the classic notion of bureaucracy, the "organization chart" of STs consists of a clear set of boxes connected by known and specified arrows. In their constructions and in the list of properties associated with their ideal organization, STs *create* a well-ordered, well-structured, perfectly hierarchical organization. They recreate the traditional organization and organization chart. In other words, if the concept of bureaucracy had not been invented, then STs would invent it.

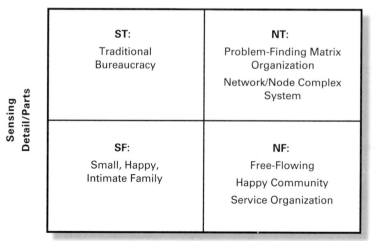

FIGURE 7-1 The Ideal Organizations of the Four Jungian Types

In contrast, the ideal organization of NTs is a Matrix or System consisting of a Complex Network with many Interdependent Nodes.[3] In the classic Matrix organization, people are not assigned to permanent, fixed working groups or jobs. Instead, as the problem-solving needs of the organization change, people are rotated into and out of different work groups. In addition, depending upon their skill sets, they are assigned to different "mixes" of jobs. All of these vary depending upon the particular problem at hand.

The ideal organization of NTs represents the extreme flexibility, openness, and complex nature of Systems. That is, NTs focus instinctively on radically, dynamically changing new opportunities and environments.

As we shall see throughout this book, the choice between different organizational forms is not an either/or but a both/and. Every organization has aspects that can benefit from a certain degree and type of bureaucracy. At the same time, every organization can also benefit from aspects of the Matrix organizational model.

In completely stable situations, which are rare indeed, bureaucracies are the ideal. But in rapidly changing, dynamic conditions, Matrix organizations function much better. Tragedies and major crises occur when we try to have a bureaucracy cope with rapidly changing conditions. Under such conditions, bureaucratic organizations do not cope well with the demands of their environments.

For instance, a major cause of the explosion of the space shuttle Challenger was the overly bureaucratic nature of NASA, the organization charged with managing the U.S. space program. It was well known at the bottom layers of NASA that the Challenger was unsafe to fly in cold weather, but this crucial information was blocked from reaching the top and what did make it to the top was ignored. (See also the discussion of the Challenger in Chapter Ten.)

In another instance, it took over a day and a half for information about the 1989 Exxon Valdez oil spill in Alaska to travel up and down Exxon's bureaucratic structure before top Exxon officials learned of the "accident" and were able to get to the site. By then, the media had beaten them to the location and were transmitting horrific pictures of the damage. In this way, Exxon was blamed not only for the initial "accident" but also for its failure to get to the scene quickly.

The ideal organization of NFs is one large, completely unstructured human community.[4] In the ideal, NFs place an extremely high premium on human relationships and on serving the greatest needs of the largest human group imaginable, i.e., all of humanity.

In the extreme, NF organizations resist almost all structure. This is because NFs regard structure as the natural enemy of 'true' human needs. They thus regard structure as stifling and subverting the 'true needs' of people. In their ideal, everyone is literally free to interact with anyone all of the time. In the ideal, everyone knows everyone else by first name.

All of these directly reflect the underlying personality characteristics of NFs. Because of their N, not only do they *resist* structure, but they also actively *enjoy* ambiguity and the lack of precision. All of the characteristics that STs value are anathema to NFs. For NFs, the ideal is to feel deeply the *spirit* of humanity.

The ideal organization of SFs is a small, happy family. Unlike NFs, who are concerned with all of humanity, SFs are concerned with a small group of people with whom they can forge one-on-one, deep, and lasting personal friendships. Whereas the S side of STs is manifested in their fascination with impersonal facts, the S side of SFs is manifested in their love of specific people.

The Link Between the Myers-Briggs and Crisis Leadership

The Jungian/Myers-Briggs framework not only *applies* to Crisis Leadership, but it also is *essential* to its understanding. To see this, we need to have a deeper understanding of Crisis Leadership.

Figure 7.2 shows the major variables that pertain to Crisis Leadership. In particular, it shows that Crisis Leadership consists of much more than merely reacting to a crisis after it has occurred. It shows that there are significant activities that need to be undertaken before, during, and after a major crisis.

Four major variables, or factors, are involved in Crisis Leadership. Crisis Types refers to the fact that there are categories of crises. This factor refers to the range of crises and especially to the *scope* of crises for which an organization prepares.

	Before Establish pre-crisis capabilities	**During** Enact capabilities	**After** Reexamine and revamp crisis capabilities
Crisis Types	Formulate a broad and diverse Crisis Portfolio.	Anticipate further crises.	Reexamine Crisis Portfolio.
Crisis Mechanisms	Design and put into place Signal Detection, Damage Containment, Business Recovery, and Crisis Learning Mechanisms.	Implement Damage Containment and Business Recovery functions.	Reexamine Signal Detection, etc. Mechanisms.
Crisis Systems	Form and train a Crisis Leadership Team; implement a Crisis Leadership reward system; identify and overcome organizational defense mechanisms.	Activate a Crisis Learning Team.	Reexamine and reevaluate Crisis Leadership Team.
Crisis Stakeholders	Formulate a broad and diverse set of Crisis Stakeholders.	Respond to anticipated and unanticipated Crisis Stakeholders.	Reevaluate Crisis Stakeholders.

FIGURE 7-2   A Framework for Crisis Leadership

Crisis Mechanisms refers to the fact that virtually all crises send out warning signals far in advance of the actual occurrence. If an organization picks up on these signals, it may be able to avert a crisis, the best possible form of Crisis Leadership. Crisis Mechanisms also refers to the fact that Damage Containment Mechanisms must be in place before a crisis occurs so that they can limit the amount of damage. A common example is firewalls and insulation, which can keep a fire from spreading.

Crisis Systems refers to the fact that the layers of an organization affect how an organization will respond to a crisis. It refers also to the complexity of the technologies being managed by the organization. In addition, it refers to the critical role of organizational culture, i.e., the "buried," background assumptions that constitute the "silent beliefs" of an organization. Finally, Crisis Stakeholders refers to all the parties who can affect or be affected by crises and therefore need to be factored into crisis plans.

Crisis Types

In this chapter, we will treat only the first of the four factors, Crisis Types. The other factors will be treated in later chapters.

Table 7.1 lists the various types of crises that can affect all organizations. It shows that crises can be naturally sorted or grouped into categories, families, or types. This point cannot be overemphasized. Research has demonstrated repeatedly that virtually all crises can be sorted into the general categories shown in Table 7.1.[5] *Within* each general family or type, each of the specific crises shares strong similarities. On the other hand, there are sharp differences *between* the categories.

MAJOR LESSONS

Research has demonstrated a number of critical lessons with regard to forming a Crisis Portfolio.[6]

Lesson 7.1: Prepare for *at Least One* Crisis in Each Crisis Family

Research has demonstrated how the best organizations plan, prepare for, and think about major crises. The first lesson is that they attempt to prepare *for at least one crisis* in *each* of the families. This finding is especially critical.

Most organizations consider only one or two families or types. Most organizations consider and prepare for Natural Disasters such as fires, earthquakes, and floods. This is due to the fact that natural disasters occur with great frequency. It is also due to the fact that they strike all organizations equally, so they are the least threatening to their "collective ego." For instance, earthquakes happen equally to everyone who is located in a high-impact earthquake zone. Furthermore, since one can neither predict nor prevent earthquakes, there is not the blame associated with them as there is with human-caused crises such as workplace violence that call for special human vigilance and mitigation.

Table 7-1   Major Crisis Types/Risks

Economic	Informational	Physical (Loss of key plants and facilities)	Human Resource
Labor strikes	Loss of proprietary and confidential information	Loss of key equipment, plants, and material supplies	Loss of key executives
Labor unrest			Loss of key personnel
Labor shortage	False information		
Major decline in stock price and fluctuations	Tampering with computer records	Breakdowns of key equipment, plants, etc.	Rise in absenteeism
Market crash	Loss of key computer information with regard to customers, suppliers, etc.	Loss of key facilities	Rise in vandalism and accidents
Decline in major earnings		Major plant disruptions	Workplace violence
	Y2K		

Reputational	Psychopathic Acts	Natural Disasters
Slander	Product tampering	Earthquake
Gossip	Kidnapping	Fire
Sick jokes	Hostage taking	Floods
Rumors	Terrorism	Explosions
Damage to corporate reputation	Workplace violence	Typhoons
Tampering with corporate logos		Hurricanes

Nonetheless, even earthquakes have a degree of human blame or responsibility associated with them. Even though we can neither predict nor prevent earthquakes, humans are still charged with designing buildings that will withstand the quakes' worst effects. Humans are also charged with designing recovery efforts for the victims of earthquakes.

In the past few years, earthquakes in Turkey and Venezuela demonstrated tragically that even those crises that are due solely to "acts of Nature" still have a strong human component. In Turkey, the failure to design apartment complexes that were strong enough led not only to their collapse, but also to the deaths and the injuries of hundreds of occupants. Mother Nature may produce earthquakes, but humans contribute to their worst effects through shoddy, irresponsible, and even criminal actions, as was the case in Turkey through the poor structural design of apartment buildings.

Lesson 7.2: It Is Not Sufficient to Prepare for Crises That Are Normal in an Industry

If organizations broaden their preparations for crises other than natural disasters, more often than not it is for "core," or normal disasters specific to their industry.[7] For instance, one rarely has to prod the members of the chemical industry to prepare for explosions and fires, since such occurrences are part of the industry's day-to-day operating experience. Such occurrences are a natural part of the territory, so to speak. No one has to prod fast-food companies to prepare for food contamination and poisoning since such incidents are part of their day-to-day operating experience.

Lesson 7.3: Prepare for the Simultaneous Occurrence of Multiple Crises

One does have to prod organizations continually to consider the occurrence of crises from any and all of the families in Table 7.1, especially their *simultaneous occurrence*. Crises occur not only because of what an organization knows, anticipates, and plans for, but also because of what the organization does *not* know and anticipate. Even if one has prepared for a particular type of crisis and a specific form of it, crises will still occur because of constantly emerging new environmental factors that give a new wrinkle to old forms.

Unanticipated crises constitute a great threat. Big Picture planning allows a company to prepare for such crises. It is not only the crises that one has planned and prepared for that constitute a threat, but it is especially the crises that one has never even considered or thought about that constitute an even worse threat. This is precisely why Big Picture thinking is so important. By definition, Big Picture thinkers "see the Big Picture." On the other hand, Detail-Thing people focus on specifics and details. While details are certainly important in Crisis Leadership, as they are in all human activities, they are only important after one has seen the Big Picture and "connected the dots." Planners should pick at least one crisis in each category and consider how they could *all occur simultaneously* or *set off a chain reaction*. This was what the executive described in Chapter Two did. (The fact that all crises are the product of another crisis and set off a chain reaction of additional crises is also the source of the tremendous uncertainty discussed in Chapter Four.)

The Myers-Briggs Personality Test allows one to see why the composition of a Crisis Leadership Team (CLT) is especially important. Indeed, it is strongly recommended that the head of a CLT *not* be a Detail-Thing or Detail-People person. This is not because such personality types do not have an important role to play in Crisis Leadership. They do, but not as the leader of a CLT. Instead, the leader must be a combination of Big Picture–Thing and Big Picture–People. This means that one must first focus on seeing the broad range of scope of crises that an organization needs to prepare for, and only then focus on the details of preparation. In this sense, *all* of the various Jungian/Myers-Briggs types have a role to play in Crisis Leadership.

If the initial Crisis Portfolio that an organization constructs is narrow, then everything that follows from it will suffer. This is why it is of extreme importance to have a broad framework with regard to Crisis Leadership instead of plunging immediately into details. In contrast, most books dealing with Crisis Management quickly become very Detail oriented, or S. They assume that one already knows what the problem is. For instance, they plunge immediately into the details of Business Recovery. While these details *are* important, one needs a map of the bigger territory before getting down to the details.

Lesson 7.4: The Purpose of Definitions Are to Guide, Not Predict

Up to this point, we have avoided defining the term "crisis." While definitions are important, they are important only with regard to the purpose they serve. It is not possible to give a precise definition of a crisis because it is not possible to predict with certainty how a crisis will occur, when, and why. If the purpose of a definition is to confer "predictive capability," then this type of definition is not possible in the realm of Crisis Leadership. Once again, one sees the need for Big Picture thinking. One must be able to tolerate the vagueness associated with crises. (Recall from Chapter 4 that the first element in the general pattern associated with all crises is a tremendous amount of uncertainty.)

One of the main purposes of Crisis Leadership is to act in the absence of and in advance of complete or perfect "prediction." By the time one knows everything there is to know, i.e., when one has Detail-Thing knowledge, it may be too late to act effectively.

Nonetheless, one can give a "guiding definition" of a crisis. A crisis is an event that affects or has the potential to affect the *whole* organization. If something affects only a small part of an organization, it may not be a crisis. In order for a crisis to result, it must exact a *major toll* on the lives, property, financial earnings, reputation, and general well-being of an organization. More often than not, all of these occur simultaneously. A crisis is something that "cannot be contained completely within the walls of an organization." Once again, we see the Big Picture aspects or qualities of a crisis.

A few crises have the potential to destroy the organization. One example is the Barron's Bank crisis of the mid-1990s. The bank went bankrupt because of the loan actions of an unsupervised manager who engaged in highly risky trades. The recent Firestone and Ford Motor Company tire crisis demonstrates the fact that a major crisis often exacts a tremendous financial cost as well. The crisis has cost each company over a billion dollars.

As of the writing of this book, it is highly probable that both Enron and Arthur Andersen may cease to exist. Thus, it is not out of the realm of possibility that a crisis stands to destroy an organization.

Lesson 7.5: Every Type of Crisis Can Happen to Every Organization

Every organization needs to plan for the occurrence of at least one crisis in each of the various families because *each type can happen to every organization*. In addition, all of the types must be considered broadly, and not literally. Consider, for instance, product tampering.

Lesson 7.6: No Type of Crisis Should Be Taken Literally

Product tampering does not apply only to food or to pharmaceutical organizations. All organizations have a form of product tampering that applies specifically to them. An example is the following: Computers are an integral part of every organization. The true value of computers is not the cost of the hardware or software. The true value is the information they contain with regard to customers and other key stakeholders. If a person tampered with an organization's key records, then one's products and services could be seriously affected.

An interesting example is that of the famous French manufacturer of encyclopedias, LaRousse. The French are avid eaters of mushrooms. At particular times of the year, they literally go into the forest with LaRousse encyclopedias at their sides.

One section of the encyclopedia has facing pages showing mushrooms that are safe to eat and those that are not safe. For some unknown reason, whether intentional or unintentional, the labels on the two pages were reversed. The "safe mushrooms" were labeled "unsafe," and vice versa. LaRousse had to recall the volumes at considerable cost. A few people got seriously ill, but no one died.

This is a prominent example of "product tampering." The moral should be absolutely clear: *any* or *all* of the types of crisis are ignored at an organization's extreme peril.

Lesson 7.7: Tampering is the Most Generic Form or Type of All Crises

Tampering is the most important of all the various types of crises. Tampering significantly alters the properties of information, an object, a person, or a product. In other words, tampering converts properties that are acceptable and safe into those that are unacceptable and dangerous. Every one of the crises in Table 7.1 can be viewed as a particular form of tampering. This is because the properties of a product, information, or system are being changed. The point is that tampering applies not just to products, but to everything connected with an organization.

Lesson 7.8: No Crisis Ever Happens as One Plans for It; Therefore, Thinking about the Unthinkable Is More Important Than Crisis Plans Per Se

One does not have to prepare for every specific type of crisis within each of the families. If this were required, the task of Crisis Leadership would be hopeless. Instead, it has been found that "within limits" it is acceptable to prepare merely for the occurrence of *at least one type within each of the families.*[8]

The reasoning is as follows: if no crisis ever happens exactly as one plans for it, then the critical thing is doing one's best to "think about the unthinkable" *prior to* its occurrence. Such thinking makes one much more able to think on one's feet and recover faster. The fact that one has anticipated the unthinkable means that one will not be paralyzed when it occurs.

If each type of crisis shares strong similarities with the others in its family, all that really matters is that one has given serious consideration to each of the families. This is not to say that over time one should not attempt to prepare for a broader range of crises both within and across the families. It merely means that to start on the difficult road of Crisis Leadership, it is not necessary to prepare for everything simultaneously, which is impossible. In fact, attempting to prepare for everything all at once may lead one to abandon Crisis Leadership altogether. One can unwittingly prove to oneself that the task is hopeless when it is not.

Lesson 7.9: Traditional Risk Analysis Is Both Dangerous and Misleading

Traditional Risk Analysis mainly selects for consideration only those crises that one has already experienced or with which one is already familiar. This is one of the reasons why I am extremely critical of traditional Risk Analysis, and I counsel against it. In effect, traditional Risk Analysis or Risk Management is limited by the fact that it is too ST. It is too narrowly rooted in Detail-Thing thinking.[9]

As I noted in Chapter Two, traditional Risk Analysis or Management leads one to construct models of the probability of the occurrence of different risks. These probabilities are generally based on historical data with respect to the actual occurrence of past crises or on various theoretical models. The models traditionally give high weight or ranking to certain types of crises for which one should prepare, and low weight or low probability to others. The fallacy behind this procedure is that it is precisely those crises that have *not* occurred that need to be considered.

One is caught in a vicious loop in traditional Risk Analysis. One does not prepare for something until it has already happened, and by then it may be too late for the organization to recover from the crisis. The crises that an organization is not prepared for have as great a potential to destroy it as the ones for which it thinks it is prepared. The strategy of spreading one's risk across all of the families attempts to correct for this limited oversight.

Lesson 7.10: Every Crisis is Capable of Being Both the Cause and the Effect of Any Other Crisis

Another important reason for preparing for at least one crisis in each of the families is that in today's world any crisis is capable of setting off any other crisis and in turn being caused by it. *Every crisis is capable of being the cause as well as the effect of any other crisis.* For this reason, the best organizations do not prepare just for individual crises in isolation. They also prepare for the simultaneous occurrence of multiple crises.

Organizations preparing correctly for crises look for patterns in and interconnections between their previous crises. They generate *visual maps* to understand better how crises unfold and how they are interrelated (see Exercise 2).

It cannot be emphasized enough that it is not enough to be prepared for individual crises in isolation. *In today's world, no individual crisis ever happens in independently of any other crisis.* For this reason, one's Crisis Leadership preparations are not effective if one does not consider the impact of every crisis in an organization's Crisis Portfolio on every other crisis.

Lesson 7.11: Crisis Leadership Is Systemic

Crisis Leadership is systemic. As in Total Quality Management and Environmentalism, if Crisis Leadership is not done systemically, then it is not being done, let alone being done well.

Lesson 7.12: Perform a Systemic Crisis Audit of Your Organization

A person performing a crisis audit should especially look at the range and scope of the crises that an organization is preparing for as well as those that are neglected. I recommend strongly that the auditor *not* give people a copy of Table 7.1, which would alert them to the broad range of crisis types. Instead, one needs to ask the open-ended question, "What would *you* consider to be a crisis for your organization?" In this way, one gets an individual's implicit definition of a "crisis."

Lesson 7.13: Crisis Leaders Not Only Recognize the Validity of All the Types of Crises, But They Also See the Interconnections Between Them

Crisis Leaders see the Big Picture. Even more, they see the Bigger Picture.

CONCLUDING REMARKS

The discussion in this chapter leads one to conclude that one should never take any type of crisis literally. This means that there is a particular form of every crisis that can affect every organization and business. An essential part of the training of an organization's Crisis Leadership Team (CLT) is the heavy use of brainstorming. That is, each of the members of a CLT need to brainstorm the various forms that each of the different types of crises can assume for their organization.

Crisis Leadership is difficult because it calls for the simultaneous exercise of both traditional Cognitive IQ (Thinking) and the less traditional Emotional IQ (Feeling). Emotional IQ or Feeling is absolutely necessary because one must overcome the tremendous anxiety and fear that inevitably result *merely from* considering the possibility of different crises. Cognitive IQ is called for because one must think clearly and systematically with regard to the different ways that different forms of crises can occur.

EXERCISES

1. Show how a major crisis such as September 11 or Enron had significant sub-crises found in every category or type in Table 7.1.

2. Construct a Big Picture systems diagram that shows how any one crisis in any of the categories in Table 7.1 can set off a crisis in any of the other categories. In doing this exercise it is best to consider a particular crisis such as September 11 or Enron. That is, to do it in general is overwhelming since there would be too many cross interactions between each of the various types.

3. What factors would lead an organization *not* to construct a broad crisis portfolio?

4. What factors would lead an organization to construct a broad crisis portfolio?

5. If you were to construct a training workshop based on the material in this book thus far, what would it look like? If you were to construct a workshop to give special training to the members of a CLT, what would you emphasize? What would the key elements of your training program be? How would they be sequenced? Over how many days or months would you lay out the program?

6. Suppose that instead of giving Tinker Toys to each of the Jungian/Myers-Briggs groups, instead one gave the same set of magazines and instructed the groups to make a collage. Predict the kinds of collages that the different groups would make in response to the exercise, "Describe your ideal organization." What names would the various groups give their collages? How would their collages differ in their overall design?

NOTES

1. Schein, E.H., *Organizational Culture and Leadership,* San Francisco: Jossey-Bass, 1985.

2. Weber, M., *The Theory of Social and Economic Organization* (translated by A.M. Henderson and T. Parsons), New York: Oxford University Press, 1947.

3. Burns, L.R., "Matrix Management in Hospitals: Testing Theories of Matrix Structure and Development," *Administrative Science Quarterly,* 1989, 34: 349–368; Johnson, G.V., and Tingey, S., "Matrix Organizations: Blueprint of Nursing Care Organization for the 80's," *Hospital and Health Services Administration,* 1976, 21(1): 27–39; Thompson, J., *Organizations in Action: Social Science Bases of Administrative Theory,* New York: McGraw-Hill, 1967.

4. Ouchi, W.G., *Theory Z,* New York: Avon, 1981; Ouchi, W.G., "Markets, Bureaucracies, and Clans," *Administrative Science Quarterly,* 1980, 25: 129–141.

5. See Pauchant, Thierry C., and Mitroff, Ian I., *Transforming the Crisis-Prone Organization: Preventing Individual, Organizational, and Environmental Tragedies,* San Francisco: Jossey-Bass, 1992.

6. Ibid.

7. Perrow, Charles, *Normal Accidents: Living with High Risk Technologies,* New York: Basic Books, 1984.

8. Ibid.

9. Unfortunately, much of the literature in Crisis Management is too ST. For instance, while it contains an excellent discussion of business continuity management, the book by Elliot, Swartz, and Herbane falls into this category. See Dominic Elliott, Ethne Swartz, and Brahim Herbane, *Business Continuity Management: A Crisis Management Approach,* London: Routledge, 2002.

CHAPTER 8

CRISIS LEADERSHIP AND THE MYERS-BRIGGS

> *...the debate [between astronomers] underscores the strangely unsettling fact that astronomers have great trouble defining the term "planet." Ever since early humans first noticed bright objects wandering among the fixed stars, "planets" have been more or less taken for granted, as seemingly concrete and definite as anything in this universe. But the more we learn about the universe, the less definite everything becomes. The arguments over Pluto's planetary status may seem merely semantic, but they reflect ground-breaking thinking about our solar system, how it developed and the range of objects that call it home.*
>
> *Source:* David Holzman, "Up in the Sky! It's a Planet! It's a Bird! A Very Large Ball of Ice!" *Smithsonian,* March 2002, p. 72.

The previous chapter showed how the Myers-Briggs Personality Test is critical in treating one of the most important variables in Crisis Leadership, the range or the scope of crises for which an organization should prepare. In brief, the argument was that in order to span the full range of crises that can potentially affect any organization, it is imperative to see the Big Picture. It was also argued that in order to connect the dots and *not* prepare for individual crises in isolation, it is also necessary to see the Big Picture.

In this chapter, we want to show how the Myers-Briggs has further important contributions to make to the formation of a Crisis Portfolio. We also want to show how it applies to the next variable in Crisis Leadership, Crisis Mechanisms.

THE DIFFERENCES BETWEEN NORMAL ACCIDENTS, ABNORMAL ACCIDENTS, AND NATURAL DISASTERS

Figure 5.1 presented a timeline of major crises between 1979 and 2002. It also introduced the critical distinction between Normal and Abnormal Accidents or crises.

Figure 8.1 shows that in general there is an overlap between Normal Accidents, Abnormal Accidents, and Natural Disasters. They are not necessarily separate or distinct. For instance, a Natural Disaster can trigger both a Normal and an Abnormal Accident.

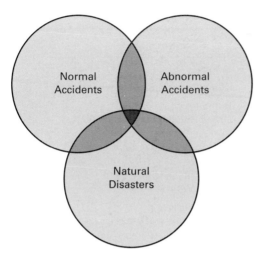

FIGURE 8-1 The Overlap between Normal Accidents, Abnormal Accidents, and Natural Disasters

Table 8.1 shows some of the detailed characteristics and differences between Normal and Abnormal Accidents. Figure 8.2 presents a more detailed listing of the different categories of crises or types once Normal and Abnormal Accidents are taken into account. That is, Figure 8.2 elaborates on the crises shown in Table 7.1.

The Myers-Briggs applies to Table 8.1 as follows: Normal Accidents tend to lie on the Thing or Thinking side of the T-F dimension while Abnormal Accidents are on the People or Feeling side of the dimension. Figure 8.2 is related to the Myers-Briggs as follows: Individuals companies represent the S or Sensing side of the Myers-Briggs. In dealing with individual companies, we break things down into their Details. In contrast, whole systems/societies refer to the Big Picture or N. If Normal Accidents represent the T side, then Abnormal Accidents represent the F side. Thus, one gets the same alignment with the Myers-Briggs technology that was discussed in the last chapter. In short, Table 8.1 and Figure 8.2 show that different personality types tend to focus on distinctly different types of crises.

Chapter 7 dealt mainly with Crisis Types from the Normal side of the continuum. However, as Chapter Five argued, there has been a shift from the Normal to the Abnormal. Our consideration of different types of crises has to broaden to keep pace with these unfortunate changes.

The difference between the top and the bottom of Figure 8.2 is simple. The top represents the *breakdown* of complex systems, and the bottom represents the *breakup* of complex systems. Thus, all of the same crises are found on both the top and the bottom. However, where the top is due mainly to the *unintentional* breakdown of complex systems, the crises on the bottom are due mainly to the *intentional* breakup of complex systems, especially as they are embedded throughout the entire infrastructure of modern societies. Indeed, the definition of complexity is that of "imbeddedness."

Table 8-1 Normal versus Abnormal Accidents

Normal	Abnormal
Breakdown	Breakup
Omission/Commission	Commission/Omission
Human/ Organizational error	Human/ Organizational psychopathology
Systems complexity/Failure	Systems sociopathology
Safe/Unsafe	Good/Evil
Inherent/Interactive defects/ Weaknesses	Create/Intensify inherent defects/Weaknesses
Faulty design/Maintenance	Exploit design/ Maintenance weaknesses
Manufacturing errors/Weaknesses	Vulnerabilities
Breaches of security	Penetration of security
Lack of intelligent design	Lack of just/Compassionate design
Failure of expenditures/Controls	Failure of justice
Passive neglect	Active tampering
Unintentional	Intentional
Stupidity	Evil

In addition, the upper right-hand quadrant of Figure 8.2 shows that when we move to the Systemic or Societal level of crises, then we move beyond the crises that affect individual businesses and industries to those that affect whole societies, i.e., the general systems, or infrastructure, upon which every complex modern society depends.

One of the key points of Figure 8.2 is that all of the quadrants are interdependent. A crisis in any quadrant can trigger a series of crises in each of the others. For this reason, a robust Crisis Portfolio consists of the selection of *at least one* crisis in each of the categories or "boxes" in Figure 8.2. Thus, Figure 8.2 broadens even more the considerations upon which an adequate Crisis Portfolio depends.

The notion of a Crisis Portfolio that we have been developing in the past two chapters is an ideal. One would hardly expect any individual company, industry, or society to be prepared for every one of the categories shown in Figure 8.2. As the United States has been made painfully aware of since September 11, the "holes" or "pockets of vulnerability" throughout the country are considerable indeed. Figure 8.2 represents a long-term ideal, i.e., something to be achieved over a period of time rather than a "scorecard" applied to the present. Nonetheless, Figure 8.2 can be used to assess the gap between what one would like to achieve and one's current capabilities.

SIGNAL DETECTION

The Myers-Briggs also plays a special role in the other key variables in the Crisis Leadership framework (see Figure 7.2). For instance, consider the variable Crisis

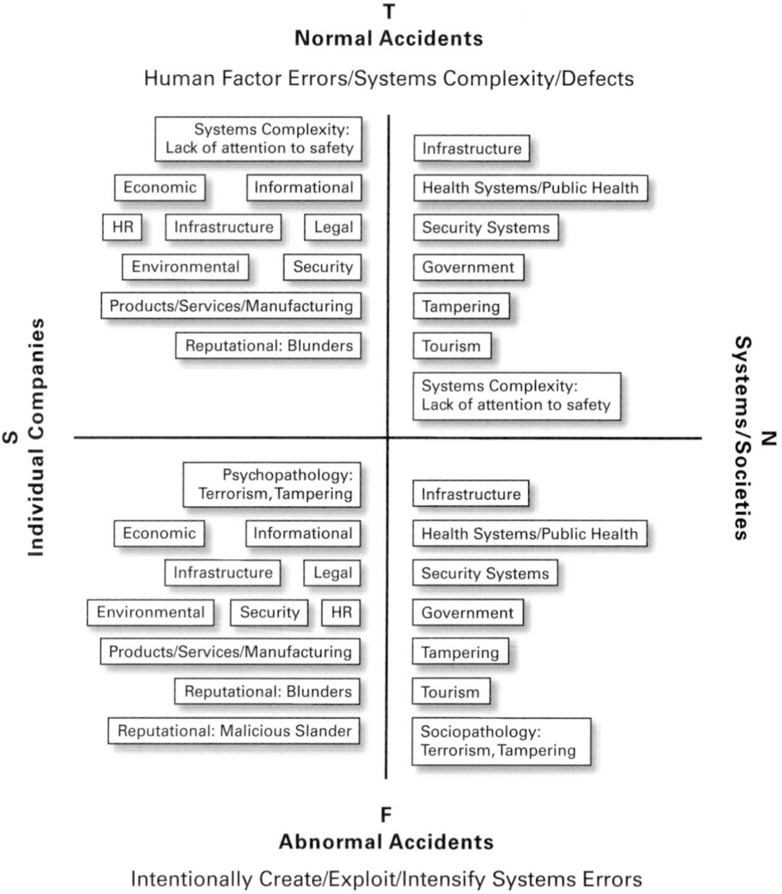

T
Normal Accidents

Human Factor Errors/Systems Complexity/Defects

FIGURE 8-2   Normal versus Abnormal Crises

Mechanisms. One of the most important aspects or sub-variables of Crisis Mechanisms is Signal Detection. Recall that long before any crisis occurs, early warning signals announce its probable occurrence. If one can pick up and act on these signals, then one may be able to prevent the crisis altogether, or at least mitigate its worst effects.

The Myers-Briggs allows one to classify the types of early warning signals. Figure 8.3 classifies some of the types of signals by whether they originate Internal to an organization or External to it, i.e., from its environment. In the same fashion, there are Technical versus People types of signals. Figure 8.3 is a very brief illustration of such signals.

The same general lesson about warning signals applies here. It is highly desirable to have a detector in each of the various quadrants. Since this is so important, we will elaborate on this point in another chapter.

By the same token, Figure 8.4 shows some of the activities that are involved in business recovery, i.e., the critical activities that must be accomplished in order to get an organization back in business after a crisis.

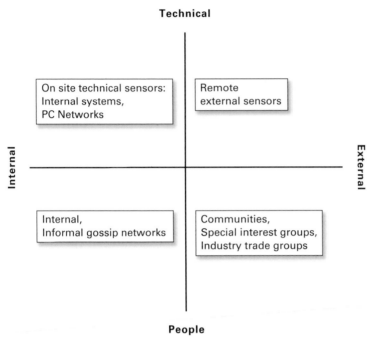

FIGURE 8-3 Types of Signals

EXERCISES

1. Give an example of a Normal Accident and another of an Abnormal Accident. Show how each characteristic in Table 8.1 applies to each of your examples. For instance, a characteristic of a Normal Accident is that it represents the transition from a system that is supposedly Safe to one that is Unsafe through the compromise or the violation of safety standards or the installation of improper safety equipment. Abnormal Accidents represent the transition from Good to Evil. The events of 9/11 are a prominent example.

2. Which of the crises in Figure 8.2 would you predict that organizations are most likely to prepare for and to neglect? Why? Which particular crises in Figure 8.2 would you predict would be the most difficult to get organizations to consider? Why?

3. Show how a particular crisis is actually a series of the types shown in Figure 8.2.

4. Apply Figure 8.3 to a particular crisis. Consider each of the four quadrants and show how a signal in each quadrant could have heralded the crisis.

5. Consider a crisis and how Figure 8.4 would apply. That is, show in each of the quadrants the kind of backup Business Recovery functions that would help an organization after a crisis.

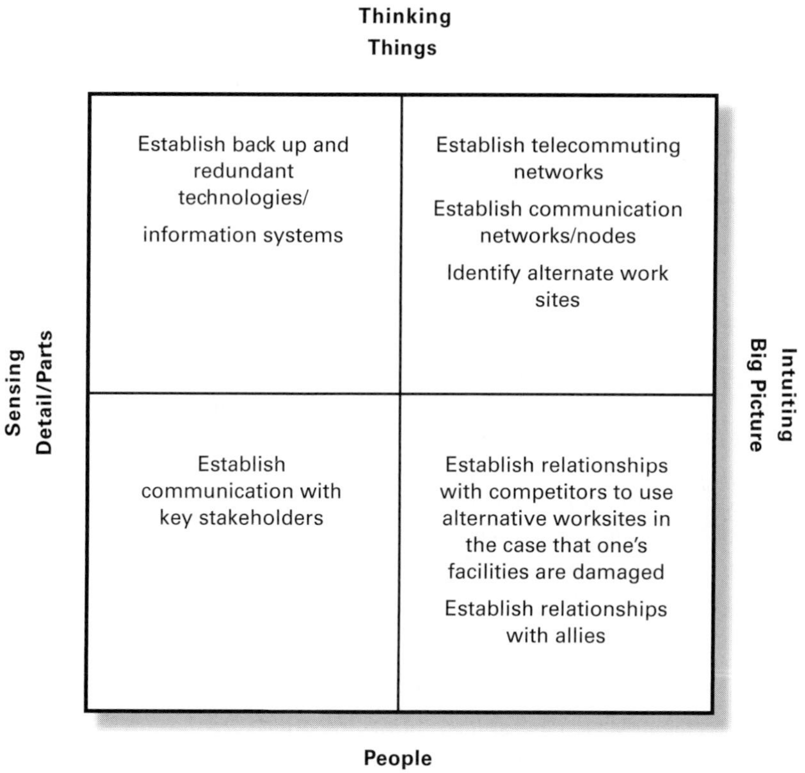

Thinking
Things

Establish back up and redundant technologies/ information systems	Establish telecommuting networks Establish communication networks/nodes Identify alternate work sites
Establish communication with key stakeholders	Establish relationships with competitors to use alternative worksites in the case that one's facilities are damaged Establish relationships with allies

Sensing
Detail/Parts

Intuiting
Big Picture

People

FIGURE 8-4   Business Recovery Activities/Functions

CHAPTER 9

THE ROLE OF CONFLICT IN CRISIS LEADERSHIP

Defense Secretary Donald Rumsfeld is expected to oppose any proposal to take away the Pentagon's control over the Defense Department's intelligence agencies, where most intelligence dollars go. [CIA Director George] Tenet, who spent 10 years as a staffer on Capitol Hill, doesn't want to challenge Rumsfeld, who is at the height of his power. Those who know Tenet say he has little taste for taking on superiors. "[Tenet's] focus is always just going to be on getting the job done."

Source: Massimo Calabresi and Romesh Ratnesar, "Can We Stop the Next Attack?" *TIME,* March 11, 2002, p. 30.

In the preceding chapters, we have argued for the importance of the Jungian/Myers-Briggs framework with regard to Crisis Leadership. Indeed, the Jungian/Myers-Briggs framework is the foundation for the Crisis Leadership framework.

Nonetheless, the Jungian/Myers-Briggs framework does not exhaust all of the features associated with an individual's or an organization's "personality." Other important dimensions need to be considered. Once we have brought these other dimensions into focus, we will be in a stronger position to explain and apply a more comprehensive framework.

CONFLICT

Conflict is as inevitable as life itself. It is a constant of life.

It is impossible for any two people to agree completely. As Freud showed, there are even deep internal conflicts within a single individual.

On the other hand, how an individual conceives of and responds to conflict *is variable.* It depends on a personality trait characteristic both of individuals and organizations.

Furthermore, not all conflict is the same. There are worlds of difference between productive conflict versus destructive conflict. Crisis Leadership demands productive conflict and is hampered severely by destructive conflict.

How individuals and organizations respond to conflict is an important aspect of their personality. Figure 9.1 shows five major orientations toward the handling of conflict whether conflict is regarded as good or bad. These five orientations are:

- Competing;
- Avoiding;
- Accommodating;
- Compromising; and
- Collaborating.

The framework in Figure 9.1 was created by Professors Kenneth Thomas and Ralph Kilmann.[1] Not only have they identified five characteristic ways of responding to conflict, but they have also developed an excellent instrument for measuring a person's or an organization's conflict handling style. For this reason, it is also recommended highly that the reader take this instrument before reading this chapter.[2]

THE CONFLICT FRAMEWORK

An excellent way to understand the Thomas-Kilmann framework is to imagine a person faced with dividing a pie. *Competing* is the case where the person *takes* the whole pie for him or herself. *Accommodating* the case where the person willingly *gives up* his or her share of the pie to another. *Avoiding* occurs when the person avoids a possible conflict altogether and doesn't give or get any of the pie. *Compromising* occurs when a person gives and gets half of the pie. In other words, the person is willing to settle for less than the whole pie. *Collaborating* is the most interesting case because it is the situation where both parties simultaneously give and get the "whole pie." In the case of Collaboration, the pie is expanded.

Figure 9.1 shows that two dimensions are critical to the understanding of conflict. The horizontal dimension represents how much one is willing to accommodate

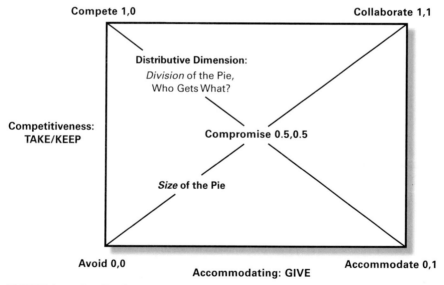

FIGURE 9-1   Conflict Styles

to the wishes of another. It represents how much a person is willing to Give his or her "share" of the pie to another. The vertical dimension represents "competitiveness." It represents how much a person is willing to Take or Keep his or her share of the pie.

Figure 9.1 also shows two diagonals that are just as critical to the understanding of conflict. The diagonal sloping from the bottom left (Avoid) to the upper right (Collaborate) represents the "size of the pie" up for distribution. The other diagonal, sloping from the upper left (Compete) to the bottom right (Accommodate), is known as the "distributive dimension." It represents "who gets *how much* of the pie that is up for distribution."

Figure 9.2 shows each of these two dimensions in greater detail. In the extreme lower left-hand region of the figure represented by the condition Avoid is the point whose coordinates are 0,0. This is the case where the "size" of the pie is 0. At that point, one neither gives nor gets any pie.

If we look at the extreme upper right-hand part represented by Collaboration, it has the coordinates 1,1. This represents the case of a pie whose size has been increased to 2.0. In other words, if Avoidance decreases the size of the pie down to zero, then Collaboration, or what is commonly known as "Win/Win," increases the size of the pie such that both parties get a whole pie.

Avoidance occurs when both parties avoid a conflict altogether; neither of them wins anything. On the other hand, Compromising occurs when both parties are willing to settle for less than the whole pie.

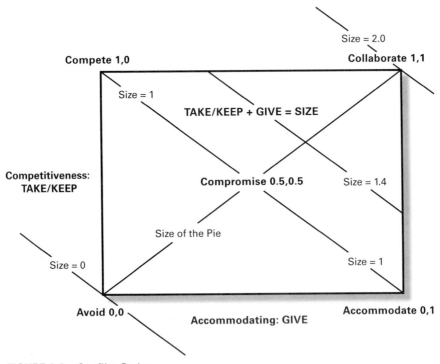

FIGURE 9-2 Conflict Styles

It is important to understand that all of these ways of handling conflict may be appropriate at times, depending on the situation. There are cases in which each of them is the best option. In contrast, there are also cases in which each is the worst.

For instance, if an issue is not of great importance to either party, then Avoidance may be best. However, if a very complex situation requires both the input and the brains of a large number of diverse people, then Collaboration may be best. The difficulty is that in general Collaboration takes a long time to achieve, which is often why many groups are willing to settle for Compromising. On the other hand, when a great deal is at stake, such as one's very life, then Competing is best. In such cases, one does not have the time to work out a Compromise or a Collaborative solution that is acceptable to everyone.

The thing that "types" or "characterizes" a person's conflict handling style is that, no matter what the particular situation, each person tends to prefer one mode of dealing with conflict. For instance, a person with a strong "Competing style" tends to approach every situation as a "war" that must be "won." Those who find conflict distasteful, even painful, tend to approach every situation as one requiring Avoidance.

Figure 9.2 shows that as one moves from Avoidance to Collaboration, one moves along the diagonal line from the bottom left to the upper right. The diagonal line that slopes from the upper left to the bottom right can be described by a simple equation. This equation is: the amount one Gets/Keeps/Takes plus the amount one Gives equals the Size of the pie. Thus, Figure 9.2 shows what is possible if the Size of the pie is respectively 0, 1, 1.4, and 2.0. In each case, the Size of the pie, or the amount that is up for distribution, increases. In other words, there is more to divide.

THE MYERS-BRIGGS AND CONFLICT

Figure 9.3 shows the Jungian/Myers-Briggs types plotted on top of the Conflict framework. It must be noted that Figure 9.3 plots only one of the many possible associations between the Jungian/Myers-Briggs and the Conflict framework. It is possible to find every personality type associated in some way with each of the five different conflict handling styles shown in Figure 9.3. Nonetheless, there does tend to be a "strong association" between the personality types shown in Figure 9.3 and the conflict handling styles. It makes sense why those with an extreme Detail-People and Big Picture-People orientations would be attracted to Avoidance and Accommodating. Feeling is in fact the personality function that tends to be extremely sensitive to the needs of others, and for this very reason, it tends to avoid "messy conflict situations."

In the same way, because of their Detail-Thing orientation, STs are much more likely to favor Competing. In a similar fashion, it is not surprising that we would find Big Picture-Thing and Big Picture-People personality types most inclined to pursue Collaboration. Collaboration demands that one explicitly take a Big Picture stance for it is explicitly concerned with integrating the views of different people. By the same token, we would not be surprised that a Compromising position would attract a mixed variety of personality types, such as those who are willing to settle for "what can be obtained."[3]

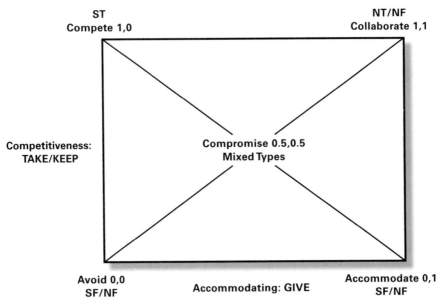

FIGURE 9-3 Conflict Styles and the Myers-Briggs

CONFLICT AND TRANSACTIONAL ANALYSIS

Figure 9.4 shows what happens if we add another personality dimension to both the Jungian/Myers-Briggs and the Conflict styles framework. This framework is Transactional Analysis.

In effect, Transactional Analysis (TA) treats "internal stakeholders." That is, Transactional Analysis posits that inside of each of us, i.e., our minds, there are "three characters or voices" that govern how we speak and how we approach various situations. These internal voices are modeled after Freud's id, ego, and superego. In the terminology of Transactional Analysis, they are known respectively as Child, Adult, and Parent.

The Child is the part of us that "never grows up." It is instinctual, moody, and governed by insatiable desires. It always wants to have fun, buy toys, and say and do bad things, irrespective of their social cost. In short, this represents a child lacking in socialization or social development.

The Parent is the rule maker, the authority figure. It is the one that says what one can and cannot do. It is the voice of conscience. It is the little voice inside of one's head that says you can't do this, you can't have this, sit still, be quiet, obey the rules, and be a good citizen.

It falls to the Adult to intervene or "manage" the competing voices of the Child and the Parent. The Adult has to balance the conflicting demands. Figure 9.4 shows that while all of the TA types can be associated with any one of the five conflict handling styles, there is nonetheless a "strong tendency" for particular TA styles to be associated with particular conflict handling styles.

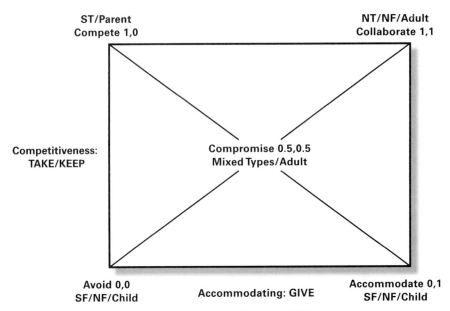

FIGURE 9-4 Conflict Styles and the Myers-Briggs and TA

For instance, we would expect that Avoiding and Accommodating would be governed, if not influenced, by the Child. This is the case when one says, "You are bigger and stronger than me; therefore you must be right. I am wrong; therefore you deserve to get what I have." At the other extreme is the Parent, which says, "I'm right; you're wrong. Therefore I deserve what you have."

Figure 9.3 also shows that in order to be able to Compromise or Collaborate, the Adult ego state is necessary. Indeed, one can say that only by moving into the Adult voice or ego state do Compromising and Collaboration become possible.

The point of this chapter is that it is very difficult to practice Crisis Leadership unless one is in the Adult mode.

CONCLUDING REMARKS

Figure 9.4 shows how each of the three major frameworks combine or interact. This combined or integrated framework is, in effect, the foundation for Crisis Leadership. That is, all of the various options in the figure are necessary for Crisis Leadership.

For instance, in forming a Crisis Portfolio, Collaboration is absolutely necessary. One has to take the crises that executives in an organization see and blend them together if one is to protect the organization from all the types of crises that can befall it. Without Collaboration, there will be major areas of vulnerability.

Within any particular category or family of crises, it may be better to Accommodate the wishes of another member of an organization's Crisis Leadership Team in order to make the group as a whole function more smoothly.

EXERCISES

1. Take any major crisis and show how each of the personality configurations in Figure 9.4 applies.

2. Show how an organization can be severely impacted by crises if it does not understand and apply the framework in Figure 9.4.

NOTES

1. Thomas, Kenneth, and Kilmann, Ralph, *Thomas-Kilmann Conflict Mode Instrument*, Palo Alto, CA: Consulting Psychologists Press, 1974.

2. Ibid.

3. I must note that these observations are not necessarily in agreement with what Professors Kilmann and Thomas have found. See Kilmann, Ralph H., and Thomas, Kenneth W., "Interpersonal Conflict-Handling Behavior as Reflections of Jungian Personality Dimensions," *Psychological Reports*, 1975, 37(3): 971–980. Kilmann and Thomas found that the integrative dimension is correlated with Jung's Introversion I and Extroversion E. On the other hand, the distributive dimension is correlated with Thinking T and F. While I do not necessarily agree with these results, over the years I have found the associations between the Myers-Briggs and the Conflict Instrument to be as I have described them in the text.

CHAPTER 10

AN EXPANDED VIEW OF SIGNAL DETECTION

Though [lawyer Tab] Turner is a sole practitioner working out of a modest suburban office, Ford has no greater legal nemesis. For weeks, Ford's 250-person public-relations department fought a guerrilla war trying to contain the damage *of documents leaked by Turner. "Every day Tab would take one of those documents and say, 'Here's a little grenade—let me throw it in there,'" said Ford's Vice President for Public Relations, Jason Vines, who calls Turner "one of those sharks out there who think they have found the keys to the A.T.M."*

Source: Michael Winerip, "What's Tab Turner Got Against Ford?" *New York Times Magazine,* December 17, 2000, pp. 48–49.

THE CASE OF THE HIGH-TECH FARMER

A few years ago, the *CBS Sunday News* television show featured a segment on a Texas farmer. It demonstrated the extreme importance of Signal Detection in Crisis Leadership.

At the time of the news show, Texas was experiencing one of the worst droughts in its history. Unlike the rest of his neighbors, the farmer who was the focus of the story had prepared by digging extra well ponds on his ranch. As a result, he was able to store water that fell during the rainy season. What was unique, and therefore newsworthy, was how the farmer got the idea.

The farmer had developed the habit of logging on regularly to the Internet. By monitoring the long-term weather forecasts of the National Oceanic & Atmospheric Administration, he picked up "early warning signals" that a drought might develop in his part of Texas. Because the forecasts had proved extremely accurate in the past, he took them seriously and engaged in "preemptive actions." He engaged in "preemptive damage control."

As he was digging extra wells, the farmer took a lot of kidding from his neighbors. Their attitudes changed dramatically when the drought arrived.

One of the major points of this example is that the exact nature of one's particular business is now totally irrelevant. What *is* relevant is the fact that whether one *literally* survives or not in today's world depends on the exercise of different kinds of intelligence and learning.

SIGNAL DETECTION

If anything is at the heart of Crisis Leadership, it is Signal Detection. For this reason alone, it is one of the major topics of this book. As we indicated earlier, Signal Detection is at the heart of the new organizational structures for Crisis Leadership. This chapter expands on our earlier discussion.

CRISIS MECHANISMS

Most serious students and practitioners of Crisis Management recognize that the best form, i.e., Crisis Leadership, is preparation for crises before they occur. Yet, plans per se are not the most important thing. Instead, the important thing is an organization's Crisis Leadership *capabilities*. These capabilities are realized through various mechanisms for (1) anticipating, (2) sensing, (3) reacting to, (4) containing, (5) learning from, and (6) redesigning effective organizational procedures for handling crises.

Research has also shown the importance of the following lessons or principles.[1]

Lesson 10.1: All Crises Are Preceded by Early Warning Signals

Far in advance of their occurrence, all crises send out a trail of early warning signals. If these signals are picked up and acted upon, then a crisis can be prevented, the best possible form of Crisis Leadership. The key point is that Signal Detection Mechanisms have to be designed, put in place, and made operable long before a crisis occurs or they will not function in the heat of a crisis. Furthermore, without the proper Signal Detection Mechanisms, an organization both makes a crisis more likely to occur and seriously reduces the chances of bringing it under control.

Because crises expand quickly, early signal detection is vital. Since a "signal detector" for one type of crisis in Table 7.1 will not necessarily be appropriate for others, one has to have an appropriate *range* of Signal Detection Mechanisms.

Lesson 10.2: Signals Are Not Self-Amplifying or Self-Blocking

One of the most important examples of signal detection is the space shuttle Challenger case. The Presidential Commission Report[2] into the causes of the shuttle explosion, with the resulting loss of the lives of seven astronauts, found that the technical cause of the "accident" was a faulty O-ring design. The O-ring was supposed to prevent dangerous fuel vapors from getting to the rocket engines. Because the shuttle was launched in cold weather, the O-ring failed to "seat" properly.

Even more serious were the human causes of the accident. A faulty organization prevented those who had serious doubts about the adequacy of the O-ring design from being heard. Their voices and concerns were prevented from getting to the top.

The case of the Challenger thus shows that it is one thing to have *weak* early warning signals of a potential crisis, but it is another to have those signals blocked within an organization. It is for good reason that organizations that deliberately block signals deserve the label "crisis prone."

However, the Challenger case is worse than blocked signals. The Appendix to the Presidential Commission Report contains a string of memos that failed to make it from the bowels of the organization to the very top. One of the most poignant begins with the plaintive cry "Help!" In no uncertain terms, the memo says that if the space shuttle flies with the current O-ring design, a disaster is virtually guaranteed to happen.

The Presidential Commission Report shows all too well how an organization that exercises its power and creativity in blocking bad news, rather than in attending to it, is guaranteed to produce a disaster. This is one of the saddest cases we know of where an organization had clear signals of bad news and then deliberately chose to block it.

Lesson 10.3: Signals Do Not Exist by Themselves; They Are Part of, and a Reflection of, the Overall Structure of an Organization

A few years ago, my colleagues and I had occasion to audit a power utility. The utility's operation was critical because it served communities that were located in extreme Northern climes. If the electric power failed, the communities had 24 to 36 hours before their inhabitants froze to death.

In performing a crisis audit of the utility, those most likely to find potential flaws in the electrical generators were maintenance workers. At the end of each shift, the maintenance workers filled out a log. In theory, the log was read by the workers' supervisor. In practice, the logs were never scrutinized. The reason was that the maintenance operators had the lowest status in the organization. As a result, their warnings were not taken seriously.

This situation illustrates precisely the essential differences between natural and human-caused disasters. The status of maintenance operators is conferred by humans. It is not dictated by Mother Nature. The roles, functions, and jobs in organizations are the result of human decisions, not God's.

This story also illustrates another important point. People are not stupid. To the contrary, people understand what gets rewarded and they behave accordingly to obtain those rewards. In other words, organizations often get exactly the behavior they reward. If something is regarded as unimportant, then people don't take it seriously.

The case of the utility turns out to be even more tragic. Linemen had the highest prestige of anyone. In climbing poles to repair lines, they almost always chose *not* to wear safety equipment. The job of a lineman typically attracted people who "couldn't wait to take risks." Part of the thrill of the job was to see how much they could get away with by *not* wearing necessary safety equipment. Thus, being "crisis prone" was an unstated job requirement! Little wonder that maintenance operators were not taken seriously. In short, they were not "macho enough!"

Lesson 10.4: Signal Detection Is a Direct Reflection of Our Priorities

A typical objection that my colleagues and I have encountered repeatedly is a rationalization that, like all rationalizations, contains a grain of truth: all organizations contain so many signals that they are overwhelmed by them. It would be patently impossible to attend to every one of them. Attending to signals would crowd out the work that needs to get done.

This rationalization obscures a basic point. When it is in our direct interest, we humans can search out and magnify the most insignificant of signals.

Consider the following. Most humans are naturally interested in finding life on other planets. The verification that such life exists, especially higher order, intelligent life, as well as contact with it, would be one of the most eventful moments in human history. Huge electronic telescopes have been set up in conjunction with complex computers to constantly monitor signals from outer space. The computers work by noticing the most minute signals that deviate from "normal background noise" that is always present in the sky. Doing this necessitates monitoring and noticing minute "blips" in millions of signals. Thus, when it is in their interest, curiosity, imagination, or security, humans can pick up and magnify the most minute signals.

Consider another example. In order to test critical features of Einstein's general theory of relativity, it is necessary to pick up thousands of signals and to discern patterns within them:

> Computers, not ears… will be sifting through [the detector's] data. Picking out a definitive signal from a chaotic profusion of bits and bytes is not a totally new endeavor. Though difficult and challenging, it will be similar to the way in which military sonar experts search for the distinctive sound of a submarine amid the many noises of the sea. Essentially, as the data stream comes in, it will be compared to a "template," a theoretical guess at what a gravity wave signal [one of the critical features of Einstein's General Theory of Relativity] might look like. Take, for example, the case of two neutron stars spiraling into one another. Of course, the exact nature of the gravity waves being emitted from such a system will depend on both the masses of the neutron stars and their orientation as viewed from Earth. So there are many possible wave patterns. To do a proper search, [the detector] will have to compare its stream of data against some 20,000 to 30,000 signal patterns continuously throughout the day and night, each pattern representing the waves emitted by different configurations of stellar mass and at various orientations. Fortunately, computers have now achieved speeds that can handle such a load. One commercial workstation alone can handle from 500 to 1,000 template comparisons in real time. For each [detector] links a few dozen such stations to form a master machine that handles the search on that detector. "They will be just crunching away all the time." …If a candidate pops up, it will then be compared with the environmental and instrument channels to see if it was just terrestrial noise.[3]

THE CASE OF A MAJOR INSURANCE COMPANY

Dr. Judy Clair, who teaches at Boston College, did her Ph.D. dissertation under the author's supervision.[4] The subject of her Ph.D. thesis was signal detection in a large insurance company.[5]

A significant portion of the business of the insurance company involved Medicaid payments. Billions of dollars flowed through the company's operations annually. Given the presence of such large amounts of money, the temptation to commit fraud was always high. Indeed, the top executives made the reasonable assumption that if they had not recently encountered a fraud scheme, then it was not because it wasn't happening but because they hadn't picked up on the latest scam. Picking up signals of potential fraud schemes ranked high in the organization's objectives.

Dr. Clair found a number of important things with respect to signals in organizations. While many of them are obvious, this does not detract from their importance. And, in fact, their obviousness may prevent us from realizing their importance.

Lesson 10.5: Signal Detection Necessitates Signal Detectors

Perhaps the most obvious point about signal detection is that if one wants to detect a signal, then one needs to have detectors! As obvious as this may be, apparently it is not obvious enough because most organizations do *not* have signal detectors.

The best way to think about detectors is in terms of a radio. If we had a radio that could be tuned to only one frequency, then obviously it would pick up only the signals that were broadcast on that exact frequency. It would not pick up programs that were broadcast on other frequencies.

Lesson 10.6: Different Crises Require Different Detectors

Different types of crises send out different types of signals. For this reason, every organization has to ask itself the following: "What would count as an early warning signal of a particular type of crisis?" For instance, a pattern of slow, but noticeable, increases in the accident rate at an oil refinery may be a signal of an impending serious accident such as an oil spill, fire, or explosion. Increasing amounts of graffiti scribbled on the walls of toilets, or an increase in the number of sick jokes that are passed around an organization, may be impending signals of employee unrest and sabotage.

We would not expect signs of product tampering to be the same as signs of the breakdown of critical equipment, although the two could be related.

THE DIMENSIONS OF SIGNALS

Lesson 10.7: Not All Signals Are Alike

As we discussed in Chapter Eight, signals can be differentiated along two key dimensions. The first pertains to the source of a signal. The second pertains to the kind of signal. And, as we showed, both of these can be related to the Jungian/Myers-Briggs framework.

With regard to the first dimension, signals of impending trouble can originate from either inside (internal) or outside (external) an organization. With regard to the second dimension, signals can either be technical in that they are recorded by technical devices, or they can be noticed by people. In general, all four kinds of signals apply to every organization. Thus, we can have:

1. Internal technical signals;
2. Internal people signals;
3. External technical signals; and,
4. External people signals.

An example of internal technical signals are data recorded by technical monitoring devices, e.g., with regard to hazardous operations in remote locations. External technical signals are data picked up in the environment immediately surrounding a manufacturing plant. Internal people signals often come from those who work inside of a plant, such as the maintenance operators in the case of the utility we discussed earlier. External people signals often come from those living near a plant who literally "smell" that something is wrong.

Dr. Clair found that if an organization doesn't have signal detectors of any kind, then obviously the probability of picking up a signal is virtually nil. However, once a signal is picked up, it must cross an "intensity threshold" in order to be recognized as a "signal" of "something important." In other words, every signal detector needs to be "calibrated." It must be set up to record what is in the "danger" or "potentially dangerous" region. In turn, this means that criteria must be specified such that if the criteria are exceeded, then an alarm will go off.

Lesson 10.8: Every Signal Detector Needs a Signal Monitor

Once an alarm is sounded, then it must be heard by the right person who knows what to do with it. As trivial as this may sound, it is not heard at all in most organizations. Signals sound all the time, but because often no one recognizes, records, or attends to them, for all practical reasons the signals are "not heard."

AN EXAMPLE

A few years ago, a brownout occurred in New York City on an extremely hot day due to an overload on the ConEd power system. Because AT&T depends on ConEd to provide the power to run its electronic communication systems, it experienced a breakdown.

Two of AT&T's systems are extremely critical. They provide the information for the air traffic control systems that manage planes in and out of LaGuardia and Kennedy airports. When the brownout occurred, the power dropped immediately. A backup generator kicked in automatically. However, as is often the case, the generator failed. Fortunately, there was a backup to the backup in the form of a 48-volt battery with a six-hour lifetime.

As soon as the battery kicked in, an alarm alerted a human operator to monitor the life of the battery. Before six hours elapsed, the battery had to be replaced. Unfortunately, no human operators were available to hear the alarm. By the time someone heard it, six and a half hours had elapsed. Airplanes were then circling dangerously because the computer systems to bring them down safely were not functioning.

The irony was that operators were not available to hear the alarm because they were attending a class on a new backup system!

Lesson 10.9: Signals Have to Be Transmitted to the Right People

Back to what we know about signal detection. Dr. Clair also found out that once a signal is heard, it has to be transmitted to the right people and in the right form so that people can take action, and they have to know which actions to take. If a signal does not relate to any of the daily, standard operating procedures of an organization, then even though it may be loud enough to be observed, people will not know what to do about it, especially if it falls sharply outside of the repertoire of known or expected behaviors. For this reason, an important aspect of signal detection is the specification with regard to what potential problems a signal relates, and further, what should be done about the signal.

Dr. Clair also found out that even if a signal relates to a known problem, there must be a clear reporting sequence. The warning will be ineffective if someone picks up a signal but does not know where to send it or if the person to whom it is passed does not know what to do about it.

Lesson 10.10: Individual Signal Detection Is Not Enough

Finally, it is not enough to pick up individual signals in isolation. In many plants, one part of the organization may have a signal of a potential problem, and another may have another signal pertaining to another aspect of the same problem. However, if these two signals are not sent to a central location so that they can be pieced together into a larger pattern, then the potential crisis will go undetected. In effect, one will not be able to see the "whole problem" to which the separate signals pertain. Because of the complexity of organizations, separate signals, no matter how loud they may be, are not sufficient to connote a problem. If the separate signals "don't connect the dots," then we cannot see a "problem."

Almost invariably, there is at least one person in every organization who smells something rotten. For example, consider the cases of Barron's Bank and the bankruptcy of Orange County. In the case of Orange County, not only was the county's treasurer, Robert L. Citron, implicated in the scandal, but so were high level officials from the Merrill Lynch investment firm. Given the large numbers of persons involved in recommending risky investments, it is inconceivable that no one had warnings of the financial crisis that Orange County finally experienced. It is also inconceivable that in the case of Barron's Bank, a lone individual, a 28-year-old bank officer, could bring down an institution with a 128-year history.

In both cases, high-risk investments were made with little independent oversight. (Shades of Enron!) It strains the imagination to think that no one knew what was occurring. In the case of Barron's Bank, it is as if the system were deliberately designed to hide signals. The young bank officer was both the executor of his activities as well as his own supervisor! Putting operational responsibility and oversight into a single job is a sure-fire prescription for disaster.

The case of Barron's Bank also shows how all crises are linked to one another. Once again, it demonstrates the necessity for seeing the Big Picture.

The investments were made in Japan. They went sour when the Kobe earthquake caused many of the investments to fail. This shows not only how one type of disaster (Natural) can affect a human-caused crisis, but also that *all* disasters have human implications.

All natural disasters involve human response systems. If those systems are poorly designed, maintained, and operated, then they can contribute to a chain reaction of further crises.

AN OBJECTION

Again and again, the objection is raised that signals are nearly impossible to read. This objection would be valid were it not for the fact that the same "noise" exists with regard to other important sources and types of information. Furthermore, the objection would be even stronger were it not for the fact that organizations have learned how to circumvent such "noise" when it is in their direct interest. For this reason, we are not calling for new standards, but rather merely for transferring the standards that already exist to other areas.

Organizations, for example, do not let "noise" circumvent the need for timely and appropriate financial and marketing information. We are merely asking that the standards used to collect and to ensure the quality of financial and marketing information be applied to signals that can warn of crises.

In the Firestone/Ford tire crisis, the fact that it was extremely difficult to pick up signals of hundreds of defective tires out of possibly hundreds of thousands does not negate the fact that financial and marketing information systems face the same difficulties every day. The point is that there is already a dedicated infrastructure within corporations for the timely and accurate collection of financial and marketing data. This goes back to our first observations on the long-lasting organizational changes instituted by Alfred P. Sloan, Jr., 80 years ago.[6] A consequence of Sloan's innovation, i.e., the institutionalization of Finance, is that it would be literally unthinkable not to collect timely and accurate financial and marketing data.

In one organization with which we consulted, two early warning signal detection systems provide an interesting point of comparison. They also provide support for our contention that when it is in a company's interest, it is possible *in practice* to construct systems that will warn it of potential crises.

The particular company with whom we consulted is in the food industry. The company, which is not merely "concerned with" food safety and food quality, also has an elaborate Quality Assurance (QA) organization, i.e., a dedicated infrastructure to ensure that its products will meet the most stringent standards. After we talked with a number of people within the company, the score assigned to the QA organization's performance was 90 out of a possible 100. In response to the question, "How much would the QA grade or score have to drop before it would 'signal' a potential crisis," the answer was "1 percent"! That is, if the grade dropped from 90 to 89, there would be cause for serious alarm. A drop to 85 would indicate an out and out crisis! This of course presupposes that, first of all, the QA system can "measure quality performance." This in turn presupposes that there is a "quality standard" against which one can compare and measure current performance. Third, it also presupposes that the QA system is sensitive enough to measure small drops in performance. Fourth, it further presupposes that changes in QA performance will be noticed and communicated to the right persons.

While the score was not perfect, all of the presuppositions or preconditions were met by this organization. They were satisfied because ensuring quality was at the heart of the business. Therefore, ensuring that the high quality standards were met was built into the day-to-day operations of the organization. In other words, QA was seamlessly integrated with the rest of the organization.

Consider the fate of another early warning system. It has been shown that a small number of economic indicators are relatively good in predicting when a country is likely to experience a "currency crisis." For a particular company that did business around the world and traded constantly in foreign currencies, the ability to predict currency crises was very important. Proprietary, in-house models were developed. Before such models could be constructed, however, a number of important questions had to be answered: "How many times did a particular, and potential, type of early warning signal actually *precede* a currency crisis? That is, how good were the various types of signals both absolutely and relative to one another?"

The interesting thing is that different types of signals could indeed warn of potential currency crises. The sad thing is that the effort in developing the models went largely for naught because the models were never really used. Indeed, the persons who developed the models were let go as part of company cutbacks. Thus, unlike QA, an Early Warning System for Currency Crisis was never made part of the day-to-day operations the infrastructure of the company.

Even though the Early Warning System for Currency Crises failed to take hold in this particular company, the example is valuable nonetheless. It instructs us what to look for in developing early warning systems in general. For instance, one of the first things to inspect is *the percentage of times* a kind of signal *precedes* a particular type of crisis and actually serves as an early warning indicator. This kind of exercise needs to be a fundamental part of the training of a Crisis Leadership Team.

Lesson 10.11: A Crisis Is the Worst Time to Invent Damage Containment

Even with the best of Signal Detection Mechanisms, crises are still inevitable. For this reason, one of the most important aspects of Crisis Leadership is Damage Containment. The purpose of Damage Containment is to keep the unwanted effects of a crisis from spreading and affecting uncontaminated parts of an organization.

Damage Containment Mechanisms are common in the oil industry. While they are not perfect, as nothing human is, the appropriate mechanisms are under constant redesign and improvement to keep spills from spreading. As in the case of Signal Detection, Damage Containment Mechanisms for one type of crisis will not necessarily be appropriate or effective in containing others. Thus, a *systematic* and *systemic* program of Crisis Leadership tries as much as is humanly possible to ensure that a variety of Damage Containment Mechanisms are in place and are constantly maintained.

Lesson 10.12: "No-fault Learning" Is One of the Most Important Aspects of Crisis Leadership

Two of the most important Crisis Learning Mechanisms reveal why the vast majority of Crisis Leadership programs are *ineffective*. These concern Post-Crisis Learning and the Redesign of Systems and Mechanisms to improve future Crisis Leadership performance.

Unfortunately, few organizations conduct post-mortems of crises and near misses. Those that do conduct post-mortems either perform them incorrectly or fail to act upon the findings.

The purpose of post-mortems is not to assign fault or blame, but rather to examine the key lessons that need to be learned so that future Crisis Leadership performance can be enhanced. Except in cases of criminal malfeasance or negligence, blame and fault-finding are inappropriate. They keep an organization from instilling the proper lessons. The main emphasis therefore should be on No-fault Learning. Emphasis should be entirely on the key lessons that need to be learned as well as those that were not learned in the past and why. The same emphasis has to be placed on the redesign of systems so that the effects, if not the probabilities, of future crises can be lessened.

Lesson 10.13: Damage Containment Mechanisms Are Simultaneously Mechanisms and Policies

It is important to note that the term Damage Containment is both accurate and misleading at the same time. It is accurate in that one of the primary purposes of Damage Containment *Mechanisms* is to keep a crisis *physically* from spreading to affect previously uncontaminated parts of an organization. That is, Damage Containment *is* a set of mechanisms. On the other hand, the term is misleading in that Damage Containment Mechanisms are also *strategic* Crisis Leadership *policies*. Thus, Damage Containment refers to both mechanisms and strategies.

A particular mechanism is not only a physical "thing" but also a "strategic deci-sion" to limit the physical and the social damage produced by a particular crisis in a specific way. Perhaps we can see this if we list the various types of Damage Containment Mechanisms: (1) dispersion, (2) neutralization, (3) physical contain-ment or limitation, (4) transformation or conversion, (5) dilution or reduction, (6) absorption, (7) deflection or "bouncing back," (8) distancing or separation, and (9) compartmentalization and severing.

While some of the mechanisms are founded upon chemical analogies such as the "dispersion of toxic gases" or the "dilution of the toxicity of a chemical substance," others, such as "distancing, are founded on psychological metaphors. Whatever the case, Damage Containment Mechanisms are both *mechanisms and strategies.* For example, in the Firestone/Ford case, both parties attempted to distance themselves from each other and deflect the crisis onto the other.

EXERCISES

1. Take two types of crises: one where the technical features were prominent and the other where the people features were primary. Show how the different Damage Containment Mechanisms, e.g., dispersion and neutralization, apply to both. For instance, in a political crisis, it is important to "contain" the damage as much as possible. Show how the concept of neutralization or dilution would apply as well.

NOTES

1. See Pauchant, Thierry C., and Mitroff, Ian I., *Transforming the Crisis-Prone Organization: Preventing Individual, Organizational, and Environmental Tragedies,* San Francisco: Jossey-Bass, 1992.
2. Ibid.
3. Bartusiak, Marsha, *Einstein's Unfinished Symphony: Listening to the Sounds of Space-Time,* Washington: Joseph Henry Press, 2000, 161–162.
4. Clair, J.A. , "Turning Poison into Medicine: A Grounded Theoretical Analysis of Processes, Pathologies, and Designs in the Detection of Potential Organizations Crises," unpublished disserta-tion, University of Southern California, Los Angeles, 1993.
5. See Clair, Judy A., "Reframing Crisis Management," *Academy of Management Review,* 1998, 23(1): 59–76.
6. Sloan, Alfred P., Jr., *My Years with General Motors,* New York: Currency Doubleday, 1963.

CHAPTER 11

THINKING THE ABSURD

Since the first case was diagnosed in Florida a month ago, almost every assumption about Anthrax has been challenged, if not disproven outright. *Finely ground Anthrax, it now seems, can form a lethal mist with no more sophisticated delivery system than an envelope in the mail. Powerful antibiotics, doctors have learned, can offer a fighting chance of survival even after symptoms have appeared. Yet the amount of spores needed to produce inhalation Anthrax, the deadliest form of the disease, could be far smaller than previously believed.*

Source: William J. Broad, Stephen Engelberg, Judith Miller, and Sheryl Gay Stolberg, "Excruciating Lessons in the Ways of a Disease," *New York Times,* October 31, 2001, pp. A1, B8.

The Muslim Brotherhood is a well-known terrorist organization.[1] Speculation has it that it may have been involved, directly or indirectly, in the events of September 11, 2001.[2]

One of the prominent brands of soft drinks manufactured by the Coca-Cola Company is Fanta. Members of the Muslim Brotherhood performed their own unique translation of the word "Fanta" into Arabic. According to them—I should note that this translation is not shared by moderate Muslims—Fanta means "No Allah." This "proves" to the Muslim Brotherhood that the Coca-Cola Company and, more broadly, America are enemies of the Muslim faith.

Is it possible to understand such thinking?

QUINTESSENTIALLY HUMAN

The thinkable and the unthinkable are quintessential products of the human imagination. What can be thought of by one human can in principle be thought of by another. If this were not the case, then the science of cryptography, the making and the breaking of codes, would be utterly impossible. While it cannot be proved, by the same token it cannot be *disproved* that for every code, there is a counter code, i.e., a procedure for breaking the original code.

We are not concerned with methods that will guarantee that we can produce every "conceivable thinkable" and "unthinkable" act that can be imagined by humans.

For the same reason that we cannot guarantee the attainment or the production of perfect knowledge, there are no such methods.[3]

The history of human thought is strewn with one flawed attempt after another that promised to deliver certain or perfect knowledge. In the end, every attempt was shown to suffer from irreparable flaws.[4]

Our goal is more modest and, we hope, more doable: "What broad strategies can humans use to think about the unthinkable and to undertake actions that will make it less likely?" Since all crises have aspects that are unthinkable, the topic is thus germane to Crisis Leadership.

THINKING THE ABSURD

In 1971 an obscure professor of philosophy, Murray S. Davis, published an article in an equally obscure academic journal with the tantalizing title, "That's Interesting!" The subtitle of the article bore the awkward phrase, "Towards a Phenomenology of Sociology and a Sociology of Phenomenology."[5]

Davis put forth a stunning and controversial thesis. He asserted that, strictly speaking, none of the theories in science were "true." This was especially the case in the social sciences.

No matter how good they appear to be, all theories in science are only approximations. They cannot possibly capture reality in all its complexity and fullness. As a result, they cannot possibly deliver perfect predictions of events. This is no less true of the physical sciences than it is of the social sciences.

The social sciences were the special object of Davis' concern. There, his bold contentions assumed their full force. If, strictly speaking, all theories were not true, what differentiated "good theories" from "poor ones"? Davis' answer was, "Some theories are more 'interesting' than others." This only raised the provocative question, "What is it that made a theory 'interesting'?"

For a theory to be interesting, it had to do a number of things. First, it had to raise up to the surface a body of background assumptions that a significant group of people held about some important aspect of the world. Second, the theory had to make the case that a set of completely opposite assumptions were more "plausible" than the initial ones.

Consider a simple example, the case of Sigmund Freud. Before Freud, the prevailing assumption was that the entire contents of the human mind were available for conscious inspection and so could be fully known by anyone who was willing to put in the work required to know one's own mind.[6] In other words, one could have complete access to and examine the contents of one's mind. After Freud, this assumption could no longer be held. Significant, perhaps vast, areas of the mind were unconscious and thus inaccessible. Significant thoughts were not available for conscious knowledge by the person having those very thoughts. (For instance, according to Transactional Analysis, which we touched on in Chapter Nine, one is generally unaware of one's Parent, Adult, and Child. That is, one is generally unconscious of one's ego states. One is also generally unaware of the defense mechanisms that one employs to protect one's ego.)

The upshot was that in order for one mind to know itself, it had no choice but to enter into a deep and prolonged relationship with another mind, presumably one that was professionally trained and belonged to a counselor, psychiatrist, psychoanalyst, or therapist.

Davis went even further. He made the shrewd observation that if someone merely replaced a few fundamental or sacred assumptions and if the replacement assumptions did not challenge the initial ones strongly enough, then the most likely reaction was, "That's obvious!" In such situations, the opposite assumptions would be regarded by most people as trivial and not very interesting.

At the other end of the spectrum, Davis noted with equally acute insight, if someone challenged in the strongest possible way *all* of a person's or a society's pet assumptions, then the reaction was, "That's absurd!"

For something to be considered "interesting," it had to challenge a person's underlying assumptions "strongly enough" to get one's attention and hold it. At the same time, one could not challenge the initial set of assumptions so strongly or completely that the challenge was rendered absurd.

In other words, for something to be interesting, it had to "whack" someone in the head strongly enough to catch their attention but not so strongly as to knock them out.

Davis did not put his ideas in the form of a graph, but this can be done easily. In fact, doing this makes the ideas even more understandable. Figure 11.1 shows that "What Is Regarded as Interesting" can be represented by an inverted U-shaped curve. The horizontal dimension refers to how strongly one's assumptions, and how many of them, are being challenged. The vertical dimension refers to the Degree of the Interesting. That is, the vertical dimension refers to how interesting one finds the challenge.

If one is in the Obvious region, then the challenge is not strong enough. Conversely, if one's challenge is too strong, or one's challenge is to an entire set of assumptions, then one is in the Absurd region. For most people, the "Interesting" region is somewhere in the middle.

OKLAHOMA CITY

Oklahoma City is one of the most important examples we can give. Prior to the 1995 bombing of the Alfred P. Murrah Federal Building in Oklahoma City, three assumptions were generally held by the American public:

1. Terrorism happens only in Europe and in foreign countries. The "heartland of America," i.e., Oklahoma City, is not only safe, but protected;

2. No American will ever commit an act of terrorism against another American; and

3. The lives of innocent men, women, and *especially* children will not be taken in vain.

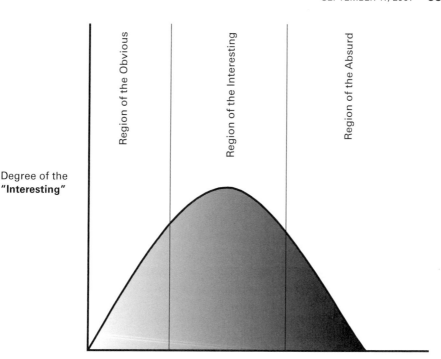

FIGURE 11-1   What Is Regarded as Interesting

Oklahoma City revealed the *invalidity* of every one of these three basic assumptions. In fact, we can say that the invalidation of basic assumptions is one of the very worst outcomes of any tragedy or major crisis. In addition to the obvious destruction of buildings and lives, our fundamental assumptions about the world are destroyed as well. This is precisely why crises are so traumatic.

It is one thing to shatter physical bodies, but it is just as horrific to shatter our deep beliefs about the stability and safety of the world. In effect, our "social contract" is abruptly rescinded. It is no surprise that when a tragedy of the magnitude of an Oklahoma City occurs, spiritual healing and renewal are especially needed. For this reason, the Reverend Billy Graham and President Bill Clinton *had* to go to the site to provide emotional and spiritual healing.

SEPTEMBER 11, 2001

September 11 intruded even deeper into the American psyche. In the case of the World Trade Center and the Pentagon, the following assumptions were destroyed:

1. Two of the most prominent buildings in New York City—*the prime symbols* of American capitalism—as well as *the bastion* of the American

defense establishment— the Pentagon in Washington—would not be attacked, let alone simultaneously;

2. The coordination required to undertake such a simultaneous attack is so difficult as to be essentially impossible;

3. If terrorism occurred, it would be only on a "small" scale. That is, only a single, small aircraft would take out an isolated building;

4. The Atlantic and the Pacific oceans are such formidable barriers that they provide natural protection against significant terrorism on American soil.

As in the case of Oklahoma City, every one of these four basic assumptions was shattered. The result is: If Oklahoma City was the *beginning* of the end of American innocence, then surely New York City and the Pentagon were *the end* of the end of our innocence.

What is just as important is that these assumptions were not necessarily "known" by the American public. That is, they were so deeply buried in our psyche that, like most assumptions, they were not clearly articulated. Indeed, one can argue that they didn't need to be articulated because they were taken for granted.

THE ABSURD AND THE UNTHINKABLE

While Davis does not provide a sure-fire method for thinking about the unthinkable, he offers valuable insights. For one, in today's world, we are no longer dealing with the obvious. Instead we are firmly, and perhaps forever, planted in the realm of the absurd.

While the "absurd" and the "unthinkable" are not synonymous, their overlap is considerable. As a matter of fact, we can say that the "thinkable" generally occupies the region extending from the "obvious" to the "middle" of the "interesting" (see Figure 11.1). In contrast, the "unthinkable" generally occupies the region extending from the "strongly interesting" to the "unmistakably absurd." Thus, to understand and to think about the unthinkable, we not only have to explore what humans have historically considered to be absurd, but we also need to explore what they currently regard as absurd.

An aside: We can regard the Abnormal as virtually synonymous with the Absurd. In addition, we can regard Normal Accidents as being "strongly interesting."

THE STATE OF CORPORATE AMERICA'S CRISIS PREPAREDNESS

Approximately four months before September 11, Murat Alpaslan and I sent a questionnaire to the Fortune 1000 companies in order to assess their crisis preparedness. The responses were appallingly low. Out of 2,000 mailed questionnaires, we received back only 48 responses! Although we could not possibly know it at the time, this turned out to be fortunate because we could then follow up all 48 with phone calls after September 11.

The results from our survey before September 11, and the follow-up telephone calls we conducted after September 11, are generally in strict accordance with all of the surveys and studies that my colleagues and I have conducted over the years. They certainly demonstrate that some of the most important information with regard to the crisis preparedness of organizations cannot be gathered from mailed surveys alone. Questionnaires don't work, because they ask the respondent to share some of the most highly confidential and critical information with regard to the organization. One can understand the reluctance of senior executives to share such information, even with strict promises of confidentiality. Thus, one cannot gather all of the information one would like with regard to the preparedness of America's major organizations solely by means of questionnaires. It is for this reason that my colleagues and I have gathered the vast majority of our information by means of on-site crisis audits that we have conducted for organizations.

In order to conduct these audits, and hence to gather some of the most critical and revealing information about organizations, we have had to sign strict promises of confidentiality. Under no circumstances can we release either the names of the individuals or the corporations we have audited. All we can report are trends, which for our purposes are more than satisfactory. The promises of confidentiality have not restricted our analyses in any way and certainly have not compromised the conclusions we have drawn.

One thing stands out dramatically. Guess what particular crisis above all others is the one that corporate executives *least* want to consider. If you said "terrorism," you were right! Also guess what is the size or the magnitude of a crisis that the vast majority of executives can consider. If you answered "small," then you were right again.

At best, most executives and organizations can consider a single, light aircraft hitting an isolated, small building. It is extremely difficult to imagine anything resembling what occurred on September 11, 2001.

Like all of us, it would seem that corporate executives instinctively put "mental straightjackets" on the size of a catastrophe they can imagine. (Read "straightjackets" as "defense mechanisms"; in particular, executives use disavowal, recognizing terrorism as a crisis but diminishing its effects.) It is easy to imagine hurricanes, earthquakes, and tornadoes. It is far easier to imagine these because they are frequently and randomly occurring acts of nature. Furthermore, we can neither predict nor prevent the vast majority of natural disasters. This means that there is not the blame associated with natural disasters that there is with human-caused crises. While natural disasters may be inevitable, human-caused are not.

All of these factors combine to produce enormous denial with regard to the kinds and size of crises that most of us can imagine. In addition, various industries also have different characteristic limitations with regard to the kinds and sizes of crises, that they can consider.

This inability to consider certain classes or kinds of crises makes it extremely difficult for most people to understand what Crisis Management entails. Consider Y2K.

Most people and most organizations entirely missed the point of Y2K. The fact that Y2K *didn't* occur was the intended outcome of the entire exercise! All of the money and the time that was spent on planning and preparing for Y2K was *not* a complete waste.

The biggest fatal flaw with regard to Y2K was that most people and organizations conceived of Y2K as a one-time event. For precisely this reason, most organizations failed to reap the true benefits of preparing for Y2K.

Y2K was a unique opportunity for organizations to look at themselves as an interconnected system. It was a prime opportunity to "connect the dots." For the first time, organizations had the opportunity to see how information flowed through their entire system and hence to see where it was most vulnerable to disruption. They also had the opportunity to see how departments interacted. This was the real, true and lasting benefit of Y2K.

This interconnectedness is a prime feature of all crises. For instance, the attack in New York City showed that the economies of all U.S. cities and states are interconnected. So are the national and the international economies. That's why the whole country and the world were affected by September 11.

Those organizations that truly profited from Y2K viewed it as an opportunity to look at their *entire crisis vulnerabilities.* They used Y2K as a unique opportunity to examine what would happen to them if *all* of the crises they could envision happened *simultaneously.* They formed crisis plans and developed systems to respond in the event that every crisis they could envision happened simultaneously. It is for this very reason that we have again and again used the Jungian/Myers-Briggs framework to show its extreme importance for Crisis Leadership. As we have stressed, the Intuitive aspects of the Jungian/Myers-Briggs framework allows one to see the Big Picture, to "connect the dots."

THE *TIME* MAGAZINE MENTALITY

This behavior stands in sharp contrast to what we call the "*TIME* Magazine mentality." A few weeks after September 11, 2001, *TIME* produced a list of major catastrophes or "unthinkables" that could happen in the United States. These ranged from bioterrorism to small nuclear attacks.

While all of these potential crises certainly could happen and demand considerable attention, they miss one of the most important characteristics of the unthinkable. In almost no case that we have ever studied does a single crisis ever occur in isolation! Each crisis, especially if it is not handled and responded to appropriately, sets off an uncontrolled chain reaction of other crises (see Chapter Four). This is why the case of the oil company executive that we considered in Chapter Two is so important. He is unfortunately one of the very few executives we have interviewed who was able to connect the dots.

MULTIPLE ABSURDITIES

Not only is the "unthinkable" squarely situated in the region of the "absurd," but it is also situated firmly in the region of "multiple, simultaneous absurdities." This is why it is so difficult for most people to devote their undivided attention, and for a considerable period of time, to thinking about the unthinkable. Not only does one have to venture into the land of the absurd, but one also has to consider multiple absurdities happening simultaneously. Unless they are trained and equipped to handle the enormous psychological anxiety that accompanies this, most people just cannot do it.

As we saw in Chapter Eight, the unthinkable and the absurd assume a wide variety of forms, depending upon which industry and segment of society in which they are located. The unthinkable also takes different forms in different human institutions and societies.

FROM EMERGENCY RESPONSE TO CRISIS ANTICIPATION

I cannot emphasize too strongly a point made earlier in this book. Without a doubt, the United States has one of the best *emergency response* systems in the world. However, we have a very poor *crisis anticipation* system.

One of the biggest unthinkables that contributed to the tragedy of September 11 is the fact that more than 40 federal agencies are charged with monitoring information with regard to terrorism. These agencies are so entrapped by bureaucratic red tape that they cannot possibly pass their information quickly and effectively to a centralized point, assuming it existed, so that early warning signals of terrorist attacks could be anticipated. How we organize and prepare ourselves is one of the significant factors in how we respond to, and potentially prevent, terrorism.

I also cannot overemphasize that the unthinkable and the absurd not only occur with regard to individuals, but they also occur with regard to organizations, institutions, societies, and now, sadly, the entire planet.

THE CRITICAL ROLE OF HUMAN JUDGMENT

As we noted earlier in this chapter, thinking about the unthinkable is one of the quintessential activities of humans. But, for this very reason, we would not expect every person's "unthinkable" or "absurd" to be the same as everyone else's.

This does not mean that the task is impossible. It is merely difficult. The fact that everyone does not share the same notion of what is "unthinkable" or "absurd" *is* a fundamental aspect of the very phenomenon we are studying.

Thinking the unthinkable is a premiere case of the exercise of human judgment. For instance, to challenge "all" of a person's, an institution's, or a society's basic assumptions is not equivalent to the sheer number of the assumptions that are being challenged. Instead, it is a question as to whether the "most critical," or the "most fundamental," assumptions are being contested. Of course, these are primarily matters of judgment, which is precisely why dealing with the "unthinkable" and the "absurd" is difficult.

In strictly quantitative terms, the fact that only four planes were simultaneously involved in a threat against America is a small number. From another perspective, "four" is "large" in that it represented an unprecedented and coordinated attack of "immense size."

I am not making the presumption that one person's "unthinkable" or "absurd" is another's. These matters are subject to considerable debate. The critical point is that without at least one person raising what he or she thinks is unthinkable, the debate will not get started in the first place. For this reason, I am not necessarily asking the reader to agree with everything that I have judged to be unthinkable or absurd.

Instead, this book will have accomplished its job if it has provoked the reader to uncover and challenge his or her own "unthinkables" and "absurdities."

Mental Judo

There are no mechanical procedures, or formulas, for accomplishing what we call "mental judo," i.e., flipping assumptions on their head. Learning the art of thinking the unthinkable involves learning from real-life examples.

In World War II, the designers of military aircraft were faced with the perplexing problem of where to place the right amount of armor to improve the survival rate of Allied planes. Early in the war, Allied aircraft were being shot down at unacceptably high rates.

One could not place armor everywhere because the planes would be too heavy to fly. The critical question became, "Where should one place additional armor so as to strengthen the aircraft, but not to weigh them down so that they couldn't fly?"

After months of struggling with this problem, a young engineer hit upon a novel approach. He created huge mock-ups of Allied planes. Everywhere that bullets had pierced the armor, he made a mark with a grease pencil. The mock-ups were very quickly covered with pencil marks.

After looking at the patterns and musing over them, the engineer suddenly hit upon a solution. He reasoned as follows: "Since we are only seeing those planes that have returned safely from battle, we should strengthen the planes where we are *not* seeing any bullet holes! These are precisely the places where planes are being hit such that they are not returning!"

Almost immediately after the Allies began putting armor where there were no bullet holes, the numbers of planes returning safely went up dramatically. At the same time, bullet holes began appearing in places where they had not been observed before.

The solution depended basically on flipping assumptions completely on their head. Do *not* strengthen the planes where one is observing bullet holes!

CONCLUDING REMARKS

What happened in New York City can be thought of as the conjunction of two previous "unthinkables" and their magnification to a degree thought previously improbable. If one puts "hijacking" and "suicide or car bombings" together, the result is the New York City and Pentagon attacks. Previous cases of hijacking were largely confined to commandeering a plane and getting the pilot to fly to a desired destination. In the same manner, previous car bombings were confined largely to particular sites. Thus, by "merely joining together" two previous "unthinkables," as well as magnifying their intensity, the result was an even bigger, and even more improbable, unthinkable.

New types of the unthinkable can be arrived at merely by putting together previously known forms and increasing their impact. Of course, there are many more ways of thinking about the unthinkable that are not as straightforward or as obvious. For instance, consider Table 8.1 and Figure 8.2. One of the easiest ways to think about the unthinkable is to consider how a terrorist or terrorists can tamper with what is presumed to be safe. By the same token, another way is to consider how what is generally considered to be "good" can be converted into "evil." Thus, for example, if a terrorist were to tamper with Cipro or flu vaccines, then the very things that one takes for protection against evil could actually be used as an agent of its dissemination. No one is more aware than the author that merely to state such thoughts in black and white is extremely distasteful. Nonetheless, it is important to think such unpalatable thoughts if one is to anticipate future such crises.

As ugly as such thoughts may be, thinking about the unthinkable means literally jumping out of the mental blinders and confines that we have placed around our minds. It means seeing tall buildings as "vertical coffins." It means envisioning airplanes as "flying bombs."

The issue is not whether we can think the unthinkable. Rather, it is whether we have the courage and the will to do so.

At its best, thinking about the unthinkable is an exercise in controlled paranoia. It is an exercise in controlled outrageousness. It is nothing less than an oxymoron on a monumental scale.

EXERCISES

1. List as many unthinkables as you can. List as many absurd crises or issues as you can. Show how the two categories are related.

2. List as many assumptions as you can that you believe that before the occurrence of Enron were taken for granted by the top executives of both Enron and Arthur Andersen. After Enron collapsed, which assumptions were generally invalidated?

3. Within an organization, who should be involved in performing the exercise of thinking about the unthinkable? Who should not? Why?

4. What are the hidden dangers in conceptualizing and disseminating ways to think about the unthinkable? What if the "enemy" takes the results of our exercises and does more damage with it than we can do good? Can one become "evil" by thinking and planning in this way? Could we become madmen?

5. How do we achieve a balance that keeps us emotionally healthy even as we become more paranoid?

6. What is the emotional counterpart to the unthinkable? Is it the "unfeelable?" Is there such a thing?

NOTES

1.   Dekmejian, R. Hrair, *Islam and Revolution: Fundamentalism in the Arab World,* Syracuse, NY: Syracuse University Press, 1985.

2.   Rubenstein, Richard E., *Alchemists of Revolution: Terrorism in the Modern World,* New York: Basic Books, 1987.

3.   See Mitroff, Ian I., and Linstone, Harold A., *The Unbounded Mind: Breaking the Chains of Traditional Business Thinking,* New York: Oxford University Press, 1993.

4.   Ibid.

5.   Davis, Murray S., "That's Interesting! Towards a Phenomenology of Sociology and a Sociology of Phenomenology," *Philosophy of the Social Sciences,* December 1971, 4: 309–344.

6.   See Mitchell, Steven A., and Black, Margaret J., *Freud and Beyond: A History of Modern Psychoanalytic Thought,* New York: Basic Books, 1995.

CHAPTER 12

THE VITAL IMPORTANCE OF SPIRITUALITY IN CRISIS LEADERSHIP

In the midst of danger, you feel suddenly cared for and protected. *The spirit is being revealed through fight or flight.*

You deeply fear a crisis in your personal life, but when it comes, you experience a sudden calm. *The spirit is being revealed through restful awareness.*

A stranger makes you feel a sudden rush of love. *The spirit is being revealed through the visionary response.*

An infant or young child looks into your eyes, and for a second you believe that an old soul is looking at you. *The spirit is being revealed through intuition.*

Looking at the sky, you have a sense of infinite space. *The spirit is being revealed through unity.*

Source: Deepak Chopra, *How to Know God: The Soul's Journey into the Mystery of Mysteries,* New York: Three Rivers Press, 2000, p.15.

The design of an organization that is crisis prepared—in effect, a Crisis Learning Organization—goes well beyond the framework that this book has presented. While the framework is certainly important, something far more profound is required: ethical and spiritual leadership.

As we saw in the last chapter, one of the worst outcomes of a crisis is the collapse of fundamental assumptions about the world. In effect, this collapse is an existential and a spiritual crisis of the first order. With one tremendous explosion, one's very meaning is pulled from one's existence. The rebuilding of new assumptions that will allow us to confront the future—to carry on—is the task of spirituality.

THE CONTRIBUTION OF KEN WILBER

Ken Wilber is rightly acknowledged for his seminal works in spirituality and human development.[1] However, the contribution of his work to Crisis Leadership—management in general—has been virtually unexplored. This is unfortunate indeed, for an important framework by Wilber is especially helpful in understanding the framework for Crisis Leadership that we have developed in this book.

THE FOURFOLD FRAMEWORK FOR UNDERSTANDING AND DEFINING THE SELF

Wilber's framework is easily explained in terms of a simple diagram (see Figure 12.1). The framework is the result of years of study of various typologies for both explaining and understanding literally every facet of human experience, from the earliest stages of childhood development to the latter stages of "transpersonal" or spiritual progression. As a result of his enormous pioneering work in comparing "developmental hierarchies" in both the East and West, it was Wilber's genius to see that there was a common framework cut across the various approaches that anthropologists, biologists, philosophers, psychologists, and sociologists had developed.

The horizontal line in Figure 12.1 refers to whether what we experience and define as "human" comes from one's emotions "deep inside" or whether it comes from what is outside of us. A slightly different interpretation is whether what we regard as human is based on external objects and things that can be observed "objectively" by scientists, or whether what is human can be known only through emotions and feelings that have to be experienced "deep within a person."

The vertical dimension is much more straightforward and easier to comprehend. The top of the vertical line—the individual—refers to whether in defining what is human we focus on the individual or on the larger society, of which every individual is

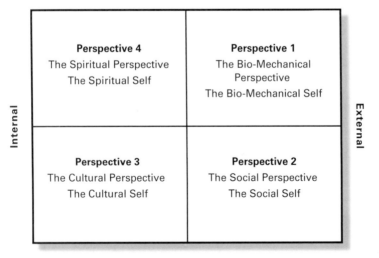

FIGURE 12-1 The Fourfold Framework

a part. The vertical line corresponds to the differences between those who focus on individual parts or details (the top) or those who focus on the larger picture (the bottom).

THE SELF AND THE ORGANIZATION

In order to give a better understanding of the framework, let us show how each of the four quadrants in Figure 12.1 leads to a different perspective on what it means to be human, or what we term The Self. By "The Self," we mean not only individuals, but also whole groups and organizations of people. Thus, The Self is equally applicable to the Organization. In effect, each quadrant in Figure 12.1 leads to a different way of defining who and what is human, and it shows where different forms of IQ are involved. As a result, it gives at least four perspectives on the design of human organizations.

In recent years, psychologists have "discovered" that there are many different forms of intelligence, or IQ.[2] In effect, in addition to traditional IQ, or Cognitive IQ, there are forms pertaining to virtually every human ability. For instance, dancers have finely honed kinesthetic skills and hence are high in Kinesthetic IQ.

Cognitive IQ falls primarily in the upper right-hand quadrant of Figure 12.2. Auditory and Sensory IQ, which are especially useful in picking up Early Warning Signals, fall into the lower right-hand quadrant. The lower left-hand quadrant primarily concerns Cultural and Social IQ. The upper left involves Emotional, Spiritual, and Ethical IQ. Aesthetic, Global, and Spiritual IQ are shown in the center of Figure 12.2 because, in effect, they are to be found in every one of the quadrants.

To understand why Cognitive IQ falls in the upper right-hand quadrant, it is enough to understand that Cognitive IQ traditionally pertains largely to individuals.

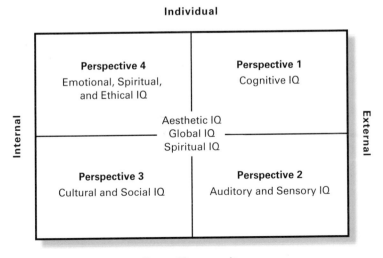

FIGURE 12-2 The Fourfold Framework

Thus, it is an aspect of the "outer, measurable" world. That is, Cognitive IQ pertains to the *measurable attributes* of individuals.

Auditory and Sensory IQ fall in the lower right-hand quadrant because here we are talking about the design of "specific organizational mechanisms" to pick up, amplify, and transmit signals to the right people in an organization.

On the other hand, Cultural and Social IQ pertain to the internal beliefs or culture of an organization. For this reason, they fall under perspective three.

Finally, while Emotional, Spiritual, and Ethical IQ traditionally pertain to individuals, they also pertain to groups. However, since they have traditionally pertained to individuals, they are shown in the upper left-hand quadrant. As we shall see, a wider interpretation of "spiritual" pertains to all four perspectives. This is one of Wilber's important insights regarding the nature of spirituality.

Wilber's framework is strongly integrative. That is, it explains where the different forms of IQ "locate," why they are needed to "cover" all of the types of IQ, and are needed in Crisis Leadership.

A DEEPER UNDERSTANDING OF THE FRAMEWORK

To understand the deeper implications of the framework, we are going to consider a concrete example, the human hand. While such an example seems far removed from the specific concerns of this book, the example is neither arbitrary nor capricious.

The hand is so central to our make-up as human beings that certain anthropologists, biologists, and neurologists have taken the development and the evolution of the hand as the major driving force behind the development and the evolution of the brain, language, social skills, community, and culture.[3] The role that the hand has played in our development and evolution is so critical that its role cannot be overemphasized. In the strongest possible terms, the development of the hand preceded the development of the brain, i.e., cognition. It was the hand that made us human.[4]

This is not to say that other features of the body such as the eye are not equally critical. Instead, the point is that the hand plays an integral role in everything human, for instance, eye-hand coordination. In many senses, the role of the hand is inseparable from every other feature of the body. Let us see therefore how each of the four perspectives treats the hand, and by implication, the definition of who and what is human, and ultimately, the different dimensions of Crisis Leadership.

THE FOUR HANDS OF HUMAN EXISTENCE

Although most of us don't think of it as such, everyone has four hands! This does not mean that we literally have four hand-like appendages protruding from our upper torsos. It means that there are at least four different interpretations and perspectives with regard to the meaning of the hand. These four perspectives apply equally to *every* aspect of human beings. As a consequence, they lead to four definitions of humans or the Human Self. By extension, they also lead to four dimensions of organizations.

Perspective One: The Biomechanical and Cognitive Perspective

Perspective One is the Biomechanical. This perspective is the result of a traditional and restricted approach to both the interpretation and the conduct of science. According to this perspective, the hand is merely a complex piece of machinery; nothing more and nothing less. While the hand may be a marvelous instrument, it is just an instrument.

According to the Biomechanical Perspective, the hand is not the thing that makes humans either special or unique. Instead, it is the brain. While the hand depends on the brain, the brain does not depend on the hand. In this sense, the brain and the hand are clearly separable from one another. While we can conceive of humans without hands, we cannot conceive of humans without brains.

The brain is thus the "central component" of humans. According to this limited perspective, only Cognitive IQ "matters." This perspective has traditionally governed universities in particular and most Western organizations.

Perspective Two: The Social Hand

The Biomechanical Perspective takes the hand, and any other aspect of humans, purely as a "thing" or an "object." The hand is strictly an object for scientific investigation.

A tenet of the first perspective is that only science provides true, objective knowledge. In other words, "object" and "objectivity" go hand in hand. Because science is the only field of knowledge that bases its claims on objective observations, only science provides anything worthy of the honorific term "knowledge."

The second perspective uses a broader concept of knowledge and of the hand itself. In this view, the hand is a fundamental aspect of society. In this sense, the hand is inseparable from society.

This perspective is based in part on the premise that the hand was first used for social communication. Both the hand and language developed as a consequence of our basic social nature, of our fundamentally being social animals.[5]

The hand's use in communication was essential to the production of tools necessary for human survival. As far as we know, the very first tools were produced by groups of people, not by individuals acting alone.[6] Accomplishing this required some form of communication, most likely by means of gestures.

One of the most interesting and provocative expositions of Perspective Two is Richard Sennett's amazing book, *Flesh and Stone*.[7] Sennett advances the bold thesis that the designs of cities, and by extension organizations, have been patterned after the prevailing views of the human body! For instance, in ancient Greece the prevailing view was that the body was governed by the exchange of heat between "warmer" and "colder" regions of the body. Ancient Greek cities were accordingly designed to promote "healthy circulation" between hot and cold zones.

When William Harvey, a seventeenth-century scientist, discovered that the heart was a kind of "mechanical pump" responsible for the circulation of the blood, then cities such as Paris were designed to promote "healthy circulation" of the "social body."

In terms of Perspective Two, not only is the hand inseparable from the rest of the body, but the body, organizations, and society are also inseparable. One cannot understand the body apart from the rest of society in which the body not only functions but basically exists. There is no such thing as a disembodied hand, body, or even brain.

In more general terms, a person, a human being—The Self—is defined in terms of its social relationships. In even stronger terms, The Self, including organizations, *is* the entire network of human relationships that it has throughout its life.

Perspective Three: The Cultural, Symbolic Hand

The third perspective goes even deeper. This does not mean that it goes "physically deeper" under the human skin. Rather, the third perspective penetrates the surface of everyday life to go deep into the cultural, symbolic meanings of the hand, and by extension, all things human, especially organizations.

Every culture makes use of certain gestures, hand signs, or signals. Many of these are universal. But many are not and so an observer requires "deep contact" or "deep immersion" in a particular culture before the meaning that a culture attaches to particular gestures can be comprehended.

Let us switch briefly to another part of the body to make our point. All cultures "eroticize" various parts of the body. For instance, Chinese culture eroticizes the foot in a special way. This eroticization takes the form of foot binding. This is why foot binding not only is permitted, but also morally justified and sanctioned. Foot binding is an expression of the Chinese culture's "high regard" and "interpretation" of the female foot. Because foot binding is so repulsive to Westerners, this should serve as a tip that we are dealing with a different culture's interpretation of the body.

A more general point is that the definition of the Self and the Organization is highly dependent upon the particular culture in which one is brought up and lives. In general, Westerners live within cultures that place extremely high value on physical beauty. In particular, U.S. culture places an inordinately high value on the "continual reinvention" of the Self. It is an unstated "moral imperative" of U.S. culture that one is obligated to continually "remake" oneself. It is no surprise to find that U.S. culture can be increasingly described as a "cosmetic and prosthetic" culture.

The Fourth Perspective: The Spiritual Hand

The last perspective is potentially the most puzzling of all to the "Western" or to the "scientifically trained" mind. This is the notion of the hand, and organizations, that is beyond all physical moorings and constraints. It is the "hand" of deep and prolonged spiritual training as that which is gained in meditation. This is the hand that reaches out to, touches, and integrates with the entire universe. It is the hand that is no longer the appendage of a particular individual, group, society, or even planet. Instead, it is the cosmic hand, able in one grasp to touch and be indivisible with the entire universe.

In terms that are more commonly recognized in the West, the "hand" of Perspective Four is probably best understood in terms of the "wounded hand" of Christ. This "hand" symbolizes the "universal hand" of every Christian and of all humanity. In particular, it symbolizes the deep wounding of the body that is necessary before one can form a deep bond with God.

To the skeptic, the preceding paragraphs often sound like New Age psychobabble or religion at its worst. It would take a great deal of argument and explanation, far beyond the confines of a single chapter, to convince the reader that there *are* treatments of spirituality worth taking seriously.[8] As science demands extensive training before the phenomena it studies can be apprehended, so too does the world of inner spirituality.

Admittedly, the fourth perspective *is* the most challenging of all. It certainly challenges the idea that the only valid form of knowledge is scientific. It also challenges in the strongest possible terms the notion that religion and spirituality are identical.

While it is true that science and spirituality are both capable of going "deeply under the skin," their notions of "deep" are different. For science, "deep" means getting to the basic, objective, core, constituent elements of all things, whether they be atoms, molecules, genes, or neurons. For science, knowledge is physical knowledge, i.e., knowledge that is grounded in things or physical processes.

Spirituality's notion of "deep" is dramatically different. By "deep," spirituality means the development of one's inner knowledge through prolonged spiritual exercise, such as prayer and meditation. Presumably, these allow one to go to the core of one's being. This sentiment has been expressed down through the ages in the writings and the thoughts of the spiritual sages who in one way or another have said, "The kingdom of Heaven lies deeply within."

Further Reflections on the Fourfold Framework

Those who are familiar with Wilber's works know that the framework in Figure 12.1 is called the Integral Philosophy.[9] It is "integral" because it not only recognizes the validity of all four approaches, but also because it stresses that all four *are equally important and interdependent.* All of them need to be integrated if we are to arrive at a "proper" definition of who and what is human. At the same time, the statement that "all four quadrants are equally important, fundamental, and interdependent" is a metaphysical notion. It is this statement that makes the framework philosophical. As Wilber states repeatedly, the aim of the Integral Philosophy is this: "All quadrants, or perspectives, at all levels of development." This is perhaps the most succinct and the most powerful expression of his philosophy.

No matter what the particular subject matter is, most articles and books treat only one or two of Wilber's four quadrants. The distinctiveness of this chapter is that it has at least touched on *all four approaches* to the central question of who and what is human, and thus what is a human organization.

As we have presented it, the first perspective is based on a largely repudiated view of science in general and physics in particular. According to the "new physics" of Quantum Mechanics, the "outer world" is *not* independent of the observer's "inner world" or consciousness.[10] In fact, one of the most startling interpretations of Quantum Mechanics is that the basic existence of the physical world depends on the existence of a consciousness of some kind!

THE CONTRIBUTION OF THE WILBER FRAMEWORK TO CRISIS LEADERSHIP

Wilber's framework is extremely helpful in analyzing and understanding the motives of those who would sacrifice their lives for a terrorist cause. For instance, Wilber's framework helps make clear that profound occurrences must be going on in all four quadrants for terrorist actions to take place.

Start with the lower left-hand cell. There is no doubt that there must be an ideology shaping the actions of terrorists. While this is not meant in any way to excuse such actions, numerous analysts[11] have pointed out that centuries of economic and military domination by the West have led to feelings of extreme humiliation throughout the Muslim world. By itself this may not explain an ideology leading to terrorism, but it helps to understand how that feeling fuels an ideology of extreme reaction. In the lower right-hand quadrant, Wilber's framework helps make clear that terrorist actions are encouraged by economic structures that are unable to provide sufficient jobs and generally beneficial economic conditions throughout the Arab world. In addition, the West has often imposed its own brand of military leaders or dictators, adding to the frustration and ideology of hatred toward the West.[12]

While these alone may not be enough to explain the development of inner beliefs in the upper left-hand cell where one would be willing to sacrifice one's body in the upper right-hand quadrant, nonetheless, it helps give an understanding as to how all four quadrants must be necessary. One thing, however, is clear. One cannot explain the actions of a terrorist or terrorist cell merely by looking at any one quadrant. Finally, there is a remarkable alignment of the Wilber framework with the Jungian/Myers-Briggs framework. For instance, in Wilber's framework the individual can be looked at as S, society as N, the inner as F, and the outer as T. If one merely rotates Wilber's framework ninety degrees counterclockwise, one ends up with the Myers-Briggs framework once again.

CONCLUDING REMARKS

One of the main arguments of this chapter is that all four perspectives not only *can* be integrated, but they *need* to be integrated if we are to develop those organizations that exhibit Crisis Leadership in the best sense of the term. Crisis Leadership will not be attained by "bigger and better" organizations in the structural sense. Building "bigger and better" Signal Detection Systems will not do the trick. Instead, what is called for is a transformation at our highest ethical and spiritual levels.

In the end, the failure of Crisis Leadership is a profound failure of ethical and spiritual leadership of the highest forms. This is *the lesson* that Crisis Leadership has to teach us.

EXERCISES

1. Show how a recent crisis has aspects that fit into every one of the cells or quadrants of Wilber's framework. For instance, consider the recent sex-abuse scandals that have rocked the Catholic Church.

2. Why is it important to consider the spiritual aspects of crises?

NOTES

1. For instance, see the many works of Ken Wilber. These include Wilber, Ken, *A Brief History of Everything,* Boston: Shambhala, 1996; and Wilber, Ken, *Sex, Ecology and Spirituality: The Spirit of Evolution,* Boston: Shambhala, 1995

2. Gardner, Howard, *Frames of Mind: The Theory of Multiple Intelligences,* New York: Basic Books, 1983.

3. Wilson, Frank R., *The Hand: How Its Use Shapes the Brain, Language, and Human Culture,* New York: Vintage Books, 1998.

4. Ibid.

5. See Wilson, op. cit.

6. Ibid.

7. Sennett, Richard, *Flesh and Stone: The Body and the City in Western Civilization,* New York: W. W. Norton, 1994.

8. Wilber, op. cit.

9. Ibid.

10. See Kilmann, Ralph H., *Quantum Organizations: A New Paradigm for Achieving Organizational Success and Personal Meaning,* Palo Alto, CA: Consulting Psychologists Press/Davies-Black Publishing, 2001.

11. See, for instance, Lewis, Bernard, *What Went Wrong? Western Impact and Middle Eastern Response,* New York: Oxford University Press, 2002.

12. Ibid. See also Armstrong, Karen, *The Battle for God,* New York: Ballantine Books, 2000.

INDEX

NOTE: *Italicized p*age numbers indicate figures and tables. **Bold** page ranges indicate a chapter on that subject.

U.S. military, 1
utility company example, 83

V

Valdez oil spill, 58
ValuJet Flight 592 crisis, 11–12, 24–26, 28, 29

W

warning signs. *see* signal detection
"Wartime Benefit: Services Cooperating" (Perry), 5
weird coupling, 38–39
"What's Tab Turner Got Against Ford?" (Winerip), 23, 28
Wilber's framework (Integral Philosophy)
   Crisis Leadership and, 110
   human hand example, 106–9
   organizations and, *105,* 105–6
   overview, 103–4, 109–10
   self-examination and, *104,* 104–6, *105*
Winerip, Michael ("What's Tab Turner Got Against Ford?"), 23, 28
World Trade Center crisis. *see* September 11, 2001
World War II planes crisis, 100

Y

Y2K, 97–98

Z

Zegart, Amy *(Flawed by Design),* 21